SPARKY
ANDERSON

Detroit Free Press

The Life of a
BASEBALL
LEGEND

TRIUMPH
BOOKS

Sparky Anderson shares some spring training free time with another Detroit Tigers legend Ernie Harwell. Harwell was the voice of the Tigers for most of Sparky's tenure as manager in Detroit. They quickly became—and stayed—close friends after Sparky joined the team in 1979.

This book is available in quantity at special discounts for your group or organization.
For further information contact:

Triumph Books
542 South Dearborn Street
Suite 750
Chicago, IL 60605
Phone: (312) 939-3330
Fax: (312) 663-3557
www.triumphbooks.com

Printed in the United States of America
ISBN: 978-1-60078-593-1

Detroit Free Press
Photo editing: Diane Weiss
Editing: Tom Panzenhagen
Project coordinator: Steve Dorsey
Special thanks: Gene Myers, Laurie Delves

Cincinnati Enquirer
Photo editing: Liz Dufour and Cara Owsley
Editing: Barry Forbis
Project coordinator: Michael McCarter

Content packaged by Mojo Media, Inc.
Joe Funk: Editor
Jason Hinman: Creative Director

Title Page: Free Press illustration by Rick Nease; source photograph by Julian H. Gonzalez

JULIAN H. GONZALEZ/DFP

contents

By MITCH ALBOM
Detroit Free Press

One of a Kind

Baseball loses "a father figure"

I had a dream about Sparky Anderson a few days ago. He looked old and his hair was brown, and I called to him, but he didn't recognize me. Only after I said my name did he smile.

And then it ended.

I'd been wondering about that dream because Sparky doesn't usually show up in my REM cycle. And why was his hair brown? Sparky? The original White Wizard? Then I heard the jarring news: At age 76, Anderson, one of the most colorful, charming, perfectly suited managers baseball ever produced, had died in California.

I don't know what that means for the dream. I know what it means for baseball. A mold has been forever shattered. Fans of a certain generation need only hear the word "Sparky" and they'll know what just passed. And kids, well, it may be hard to explain. Anderson didn't belong to today's fantasy league/money ball/analytics world of baseball. He was born to manage it. Not study it. Not even play it. (He was a pretty lousy player.) Manage it. He got the game. He felt it. He gripped the clubhouse the way Ruth or DiMaggio gripped a bat. He played hunches, pulled pitchers, tinkered lineups. He lived the game's lore until he became part of it. Baseball wasn't a diamond to Sparky, it was a planet. His home.

Unlike most managers, Sparky Anderson actually looked more natural in a baseball outfit than in regular clothes. If you saw him in a shirt and tie or, heaven forbid, one of those colorful sweatsuits he sometimes wore, you wanted him to yank it off, Superman style, and reveal the leggings, the belt, the cap.

You know. The Sparky look.

George Lee Anderson was baseball. As a kid in Los Angeles, he played the game with Buckwheat from the "Little Rascals." True story. I learned this in one of countless visits to his inner sanctum, the manager's office. Those lucky enough to get inside recall a whirling dervish of a man in his underwear, scarfing spaghetti, his head almost in the sauce, but talking. Or a man hurled back in his chair like a king, hands raking through his white hair, still talking. Or a man stuffing his pipe with tobacco, eyes on the stem, still talking.

With a career managerial winning percentage of .545 (2194-1834), three World Series championships, and two more National League pennants, Sparky earned a Hall of Fame induction by the Veterans Committee in 2000.

I've heard Sparky talk about the Pope ("Oh, that man there, what a face!"), an alternative career ("I woulda been a painter like my daddy"), even a punk rock group, The Dead Milkmen. Ain't? None? Nobody? No? I have heard Sparky use so many negatives in one sentence that it became a positive.

But the players who heard him talk baseball were the luckiest of all. He knew the game's DNA. Don't misunderstand. Sparky was no Kumbaya campfire skipper. He made his players shave. Dress in jackets and ties. To paraphrase Kipling, they all counted with him, but none too much.

Kirk Gibson remembers a time Anderson called him into the office, yelling, "Big Boy, come in here!... You got something to say?" And Gibson did. He ranted and raved for three minutes, uninterrupted, about playing time and usage. Finally, Sparky nodded and said, "Are you done?" Yes, Gibson said. Sparky motioned to the door—go on now, get out—and never added a word.

"But I felt better," Gibson recalled.

And that was Sparky's touch.

Anderson's accomplishments speak for themselves. (And given how much Sparky spoke, that's saying something.) Sixth on the all-time wins list. World Series titles in both leagues. Hall of Famer.

But in the flood of memories from former players, few focused on that, and nearly all focused on how cherished they felt by him, how much he molded them. Cecil Fielder referred to him as "a father figure." Jack Morris said the team felt like "his family." Lance Parrish recalled Anderson's endless charity work.

It would be fitting to ask Ernie Harwell—he and Sparky walked together every morning on road trips—but we lost Ernie this year, too, and it seems like some heavenly roll call is taking place in our town.

I know this. The Sparky I saw in my dream wasn't the Sparky we loved—nothing brown about him—and if that was to be his path with the dementia he suffered, perhaps this is a kinder fate. Better to recall the best manager Detroit ever had as smiling, chatting, lighting up a room with a gravelly "How ya doin'?" Forever young in name and spirit, forever white and bright. ●

Sparky left an indelible mark on the Detroit Tigers, Cincinnati Reds, and Major League Baseball.

By JOHN LOWE
Detroit Free Press

The Passing of a Legend

Sparky Anderson will be remembered in Detroit for lighting up a team—and a city

With his natural baseball wisdom, ungrammatical eloquence and perpetual charisma—plus that tanned, vibrant face topped by silver hair—Sparky Anderson became the most compelling and enduring figure ever to manage the Tigers.

Anderson, the all-time leader among Tigers managers in victories, visibility and inimitable quotations, died Nov. 4, 2010, at his home in Thousand Oaks, Calif. He was 76.

Anderson's death came one day after the family announced that he was receiving hospice care at his home because of complications from dementia. The family said that, at Anderson's request, there will be no funeral or memorial service.

Anderson managed the Tigers from the middle of the 1979 season through 1995. His 17 seasons are the most in club history. The runner-up is Hughie Jennings, who managed Ty Cobb's Tigers for 14 seasons in the first part of the 20th Century. Anderson beat Jennings' record for most victories by a Tigers manager by 200 (1,331-1,131).

Throughout his years near or at the top of baseball through his 2000 election to the Hall of Fame, Anderson rejected the airs of celebrity, no matter how prominent he became. He forever seemed as happy to see

Sparky Anderson could regularly be seen on the field before most games at Tiger Stadium. To a generation of fans, Sparky Anderson and Tiger Stadium symbolized baseball in Detroit.

JULIAN H. GONZALEZ/DFP

people he knew—and didn't know—as they did to see him.

On trips to New York, he didn't eat breakfast at the Tigers' fancy hotel. He'd go across the street to Howard Johnson, where he would address his waiter by name as a friend. In countless such gestures, he succeeded in a mission he once imparted to his Hall of Fame catcher in Cincinnati, Johnny Bench: "As long as you remember where you are from, you will always know where you are going."

Anderson, born in South Dakota during the Depression, said "thank you" to people for whom he signed autographs. He often quoted his father's words to him: "Being nice to people is the only thing in life that will never cost you a dime. Treat them nice and they'll treat you the same."

A sign hung in Anderson's mostly unadorned office at Tiger Stadium: "Every 24 hours the world turns over on someone who was sitting on top of it."

Anderson's run with the Tigers was the second act of a two-act managing career. In nine seasons with the Reds (1970-78), Anderson produced five National League West championships, four NL pennants and two World Series championships.

The Reds stunned the baseball world when they fired Anderson after the 1978 season, and the Tigers produced a coup the next June when they signed him to a five-year contract. Several other clubs had courted Anderson, and he later wrote that he had decided to manage the Chicago Cubs when the Tigers snagged him.

Anderson strongly implied upon his arrival in Detroit that the Tigers would win the World Series within five years. And in 1984 they did, starting 35-5 en route to a five-game victory over San Diego in the Series.

A sterling reputation

As with most of baseball's foremost managers, Anderson didn't go out on top. The Tigers didn't finish first in his final eight seasons, and they contended for first place in only a few of those years. In his final season, as the club rebuilt with youth, it finished fourth at 60-84 in a strike-shortened season.

Despite these fruitless seasons, Anderson's reputation remained virtually undiminished. He had had so much success and had become such a spoken authority on success that the Tigers' decline was widely attributed to a lack of a talent, not to Anderson having lost his touch.

Late in Anderson's career, he received the highest compliment of all from baseball writer and columnist Patrick Reusse of the Minneapolis Star-Tribune. Reusse saluted Anderson by using the manager's famous fractured vernacular: "Ain't never been no better manager."

There was a case for this. When Anderson resigned following the 1995 season, he stood third all-time in victories with 2,194. The only managers ahead of him were figures of long ago—Connie Mack and John McGraw.

Mack owned the club he managed, the Philadelphia A's, and wasn't in jeopardy of being fired

Sparky Anderson holds the Tigers record for most wins by a manager with 1,331 over 17 years. He surpassed Hughie Jennings previous high mark of 1,131 at the end of the 1992 season.

Me carrying a briefcase is like a hot dog wearing earrings.

—Sparky Anderson

Sparky shares a laugh with Gates Brown during a reunion of the 1984 World Series championship team in 2009. Brown was the hitting coach for Tigers from 1978 to 1984, which included Sparky's first six seasons with the Tigers.

JULIAN H. GONZALEZ/DFP

despite a long string of losing seasons.

McGraw, who died three days after Anderson was born, didn't deal with many of the variables that made Anderson's job tough: players on rich, long-term contracts, coast-to-coast travel, late-game maneuvering of a bullpen and a scrutinizing media.

In 2005, Anderson surrendered third place on the victories list to Tony La Russa. As a young manager with the Chicago White Sox, La Russa frequently sought out Anderson and absorbed his wisdom before their teams played.

Anderson's advice to La Russa was typical of his boil-it-down, commonsense approach. It included the recommendation to use position players according to their strengths and to avoid putting them in spots that would expose their weaknesses. "Those tips he gave me saved my baseball life," La Russa said in 2005.

In 2006, La Russa's Cardinals beat the Tigers in the World Series. That made La Russa the only manager besides Anderson to win the World Series in the American League and National League.

"It's such a great honor—he really should have this alone," La Russa said the night the Cardinals won the '06 Series.

In the same answer, La Russa said, "I have such a respect and affection for Sparky that I believe he's one of the greatest, not just managers, but baseball men, ambassadors for the game."

In 2007, another of Anderson's favorites, Bobby Cox, also passed him on the managerial list. Cox did the bulk of his work with Atlanta, but managed the Toronto club that gave the '84 Tigers a midseason run for first place and then displaced them as East champs in '85. In 2006, Anderson said La Russa and Cox were the two best managers of all time.

The two sides of Sparky

Anderson was an extrovert wrapped around an introvert. With his unceasing flow of wisdom and humor, he dominated news con-

Making light of his forgettable playing career, Sparky has said, "I didn't have a lot of talent, so I tried to make up for it with spit and vinegar. I spent more time arguing with umpires than I spent on the bases."

ferences as few could. He loved doing interviews, and he was the Tigers' foremost personality throughout his tenure. "The one member of the Detroit Tigers you would recognize if he came walking up your driveway," wrote Jayson Stark of the *Philadelphia Inquirer* as the Tigers blazed through the 1984 postseason.

Yet Anderson continually claimed he was shy. It wasn't a contradiction. When he wasn't filling his role as manager-spokesman, he didn't seek attention. By the time he reached Detroit, he probably could have made a fortune on the off-season banquet and speaking circuit. Yet in the off-season, he retreated to his home in Thousand Oaks, Calif. —the same home he lived in throughout his rise in the majors. He could have afforded a far more lavish place, but he never sought one.

Throughout those off-seasons in California, his mind apparently never strayed far from baseball. Reporters who called him in the off-season would instantly find him at full blast, dispensing quotes as if it were July. Except for Yogi Berra, perhaps no other Hall of Famer is so well known for his one-liners. A sampling of Anderson's best:

- On the chiseled physique of Oakland's José Canseco: "He looks like a Greek goddess."
- On a struggling player: "He wants to do so good so bad."
- On his fondness for issuing intentional walks: "Don't let Superman beat you."
- On his theology: "I believe in the Big Guy."

- On how any team could survive the loss of a star player or two: "You can go to the cemetery and see where Babe Ruth is buried."
- On an unheralded pitcher for whom Anderson incorrectly predicted stardom: "If you don't like him, you don't like ice cream."

Like many managers, Anderson was better at his immediate duties—running the game, the pitching staff and the clubhouse—than he was at projecting how good players could become. In his most memorable miss, he rushed minor-leaguer Torey Lovullo into the starting lineup for the 1989 season. Lovullo was back in the minors within weeks and never made an impact in the majors.

The Lovullo episode was a reminder that Anderson deserved the same assessment a friend once gave Winston Churchill: "You're usually right, but when you're wrong, well, my God."

Earning his nickname

Anderson was known throughout baseball as Sparky. Some longtime friends and acquaintances might not have known his real first name. He was born George Lee Anderson in Bridgewater, S.D., on Feb. 22, 1934. He was one of five children who lived in a house without an indoor toilet or sufficient heat. In the winter, Anderson's father put cardboard over the windows to block the cold.

By the time Anderson was 10, his family moved to Los Angeles, but he always seemed more rooted in the humble soil of South Dakota. As

Even though he was a self-proclaimed "shy guy" off of the field, many major league umpires would claim that Sparky Anderson was anything but shy when he was at the ballpark.

> "I don't know why
> the players make such
> a big fuss about sitting
> in the first-class section
> of the plane. Does
> that mean they'll get
> there faster?
>
> —Sparky Anderson

Fans old and young favored Sparky Anderson. Whether it was signing autographs before the game or taking time to shake a few hands after the game, Sparky always made time for everyone at the ballpark.

Anderson consistently declined the perks and privileges of celebrity, it was as if he remembered that small, cold house in Bridgewater and remained grateful for how baseball had given him a life of unimaginable blessings. He remembered where he was from and thus knew where he was going, and thereby he kept his common touch no matter how often fame gave him the chance to abandon it.

Anderson signed as an infielder with the Brooklyn Dodgers. The only notable thing about his playing career was that it produced the name by which everyone came to know George Anderson.

"The name 'Sparky' started simply as a joke," Anderson said in 1990 in his book titled, of course, *Sparky*. He continued: "Sparky was created in 1955 when I played at Ft. Worth, Texas, in my third year of pro ball. I didn't have a lot of talent, so I tried to make up for it with spit and vinegar. I spent more time arguing with umpires than I spent on the bases.

"There was an old radio announcer whose name I don't remember. 'The sparks are flying tonight,' he'd say after I charged another umpire. Then I'd do it the next night. And the next. Finally he got to saying, 'And here comes Sparky racing toward the umpire again.'

"The name stuck. At first I was embarrassed. Eventually I got used to it."

As he kept the victories, quotes and charisma coming, he became one of those rare baseball figures known by his nickname. It became such universal currency that it provided the title for both of his books. The second was *They Call Me Sparky* in 1998, and like its forerunner, *Sparky*, it was co-written by Dan Ewald, the club's longtime director of public relations.

Anderson played in the majors in one season, 1959. He was the starting second baseman for the Philadelphia Phillies. He hit .218 and never hit a home run. Well into his managing career, he said, "I like when they took my playing record off my baseball card and put on my managing record."

Even after he retired from managing, Sparky would spend time with the fans when he was at the ballpark. Here Sparky signs a baseball for a young Tigers fan before a game where he was being honored.

The Tigers' coup

When 1978 ended, Anderson's Reds had gone back-to-back years without finishing first. Management wanted Anderson to fire one or more coaches, and he refused. Several weeks later, he was fired.

Anderson decided to sit out the 1979 season and return in 1980. He later wrote that of the six clubs that showed interest in him to manage in '80, he had picked the Cubs. Then Tigers president and general manager Jim Campbell contacted Anderson in June 1979 and offered him the manager's job if he would take it immediately.

Anderson did. Campbell fired first-year manager Les Moss to hire Anderson. On the day the Tigers announced his hiring, Anderson told the *Free Press:* "I began to wonder if I would ever get the opportunity to work with as good a group of people as they have in Detroit, if I would ever get the opportunity to work with talent that good, and if I would ever get a five-year contract."

Years later, he wrote: "I don't know exactly why the Detroit offer seemed so right. The Tigers met my conditions, but it wasn't just the money.

"I remembered the Tigers from spring training. I remembered all those fine young players. Alan Trammell and Lou Whitaker were just coming up. So were Jack Morris and Lance Parrish. And I remembered Kirk Gibson hitting a ball over the scoreboard that must have gone nine miles. He followed that with a routine ground ball that he beat out for a hit.

"I think the real thing that convinced me was the Tiger organization. The Tigers are tradition. The Tigers are baseball history."

Anderson received the five-year contract he sought from the Tigers. At his introductory news conference in Detroit, he said he had promised Campbell and owner John Fetzer that the Tigers would win the World Series on his watch, and he strongly implied they would do it by the final year of his contract, 1984.

As in Cincinnati, Anderson inherited a young core of talent. Starting

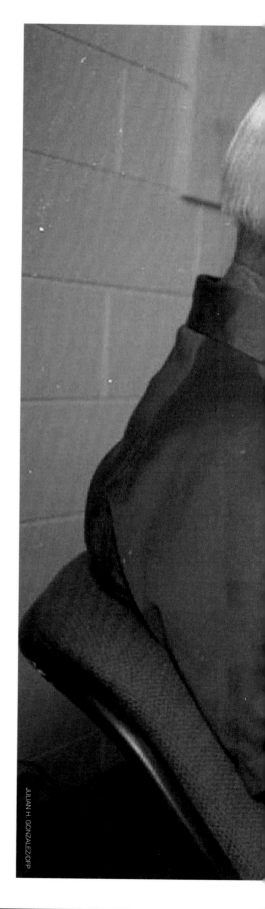

JULIAN H. GONZALEZ/DFP

Not only popular among fans, Sparky Anderson was well-liked among the reporters. Here he is seen winding down a press conference with his trademark pipe. He had just announced to reporters that he would not manage replacement players that were to start the 1995 season.

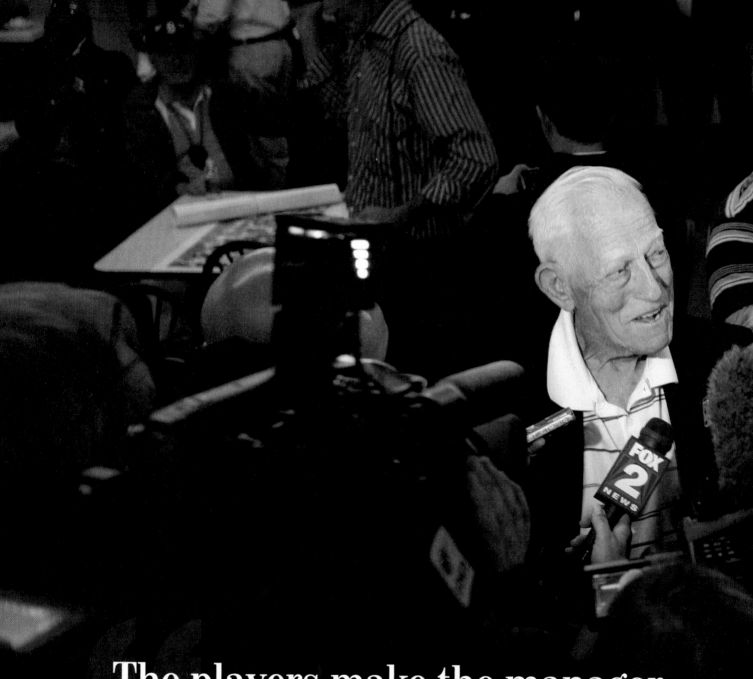

The players make the manager.
It's never the other way.

—Sparky Anderson

Sparky was popular among the press whenever he would make an appearance at the ballpark after his retirement. Here he is surrounded by cameras and microphones before a reunion of the 1984 championship team at Comerica Park.

JULIAN H. GONZALEZ/DFP

with 1979, the Tigers posted a winning record for 10 straight seasons, and by 1983 they climbed to a second-place finish in the American League East. As the 1984 season was about to begin, Anderson told a visitor in spring training, "We're not good. We're great."

The Tigers team that won the World Series in 1984 could not deliver Anderson a dynasty like he had in Cincinnati. The Tigers had one more first-place finish under Anderson after '84. It came in '87, and it was the reverse of 1984—the team started poorly but passed Toronto at season's end.

As in '84, the Tigers led the majors in victories, and as in '84, Anderson was voted AL manager of the year. The '87 Tigers lost decisively to Minnesota in the playoffs.

By 1989, the farm system had failed, and the Tigers were in last place May 19 when Anderson left the club with what it announced was exhaustion. For the first time in 18 years, Anderson was faced with a team that would finish with a losing record. "A nosedive crash into reality," he called it.

"Physically, I could not have made it through another day," Anderson wrote. "My nerves were shot."

He spent the next two weeks recovering at home in California. He returned to the Tigers and said he would try to enjoy baseball more and not let his mood be so tied to wins and losses. Yet losses robbed him of his joy of conversation. His news conferences in his office after defeats tended to be filled with short, uninformative answers. Late in his career, he said he regretted that he always took losses too hard.

His big regret

Anderson had tremendous job security because he had the respect and friendship of Campbell, who was the club's chief executive for Anderson's first 14 seasons in Detroit. Campbell's reign ended during the 1992 season when owner Tom Monaghan fired him and president Bo Schembechler. Monaghan did so as he was in the process of selling the club to Mike Ilitch, the Little Caesars magnate and owner of the Red Wings.

Anderson, who rarely admitted error, wrote in his memoir that he made a mistake that he didn't voluntarily leave the Tigers with Campbell and Schembechler.

"I've always felt guilty that I stuck around after what happened to them," Anderson wrote. "I have always maintained that when the people who were so close to you were ever mistreated, you go with them.

"I truly believe the only reason I stayed with the Tigers was because...I allowed my high salary to keep me there. For that, I am probably more ashamed of myself than for anything I have ever done in baseball."

The Tigers finished with a winning record in 1993, the first season Ilitch owned the club. But despite a high payroll and many veterans, the Tigers were last in the AL East in 1994 when a players' strike hit in mid-August and canceled the remainder of the season.

The strike was still going when spring training was due to start in 1995. Teams hired replacement

Sparky Anderson is seen here during his press conference announcing his retirement from the Detroit Tigers, and baseball, in 1995. He was the first manager to win a World Series in both the National and American Leagues.

players, opened spring training and implicitly threatened to begin the regular season with the substitutes. Anderson wouldn't go along with the idea. He refused to manage the replacement team in spring training, and thus he ruptured his relationship with Ilitch. The two apparently never repaired the rift, and many observers believe it is why the Tigers haven't retired Anderson's No. 11.

Anderson seldom mentioned the names of people he didn't like. If he had to refer to them, he would do so vaguely. He wrote of life under Ilitch: "I really didn't have a job no more, anyway. It was totally different." And in his 1998 memoir, Anderson said this about the immediate aftermath of his announcement that he wouldn't manage the replacement players: "I already heard the rumors about the owner wanting me fired."

But nowhere in the book does Anderson mention Ilitch by name.

Anderson sensed that his refusal to manage the replacement players ended any chance he would be rehired for 1996. The real major leaguers came back in time for an almost full-length 1995 season, and Anderson resigned after the Tigers finished that year 60-84, in fourth place, 26 games behind first-place Boston.

No other manager dared to walk away from managing the replacement players. Yet Anderson's abdication that spring wasn't a shock. He'd long before established that he had the courage to do what he felt was right regardless of the reaction.

"For Sparky, this was not a political matter," wrote co-author Ewald in Anderson's 1998 book. "His decision was based on something much simpler. It was integrity.

"He believed the use of make-believe major-leaguers threatened the moral conscience of the game."

STEVEN NICKERSON/DFP

Sparky was also loved by his players. Here he shares a laugh with catcher Mickey Tettleton before a game.

> "I don't believe a manager ever won a pennant. Casey Stengel won all those pennants with the Yankees. How many did he win with the Boston Braves and Mets?

—Sparky Anderson

Even though managing a team to a win is never easy, when his teams did win Sparky Anderson gave all the credit to the players on the field.

STAFF PHOTOGRAPHER/DFP

Words of a master

Anderson might have picked the right time to leave. Life in the majors was coming to include heavy doses of statistical analysis and video study, and Anderson never showed fondness for either. He trusted his experience, instinct and guts.

Those same methods led to the idea he got in 1987 in his hotel room on a Tigers trip to Seattle. He would start a children's charity at two Detroit hospitals. He immediately had the name: CATCH (Caring Athletes Team for Children's and Henry Ford Hospital). In his memoir, the chapter on the charity is titled "Sparky's Greatest Gift."

As Ilitch continued to own the Tigers throughout Anderson's retirement, Detroit saw little of its most famous manager. The club asked Anderson to a game at Comerica Park in 2000 to salute his Hall of Fame induction.

He returned to Detroit for the 2006 World Series, the Tigers' first since his team won it in 1984.

He also returned in September 2009 for the 25th reunion of the '84 champs. Twenty-four members gathered together for a few days, even posed for a team photo with the World Series trophy. Trammell. Parrish. Gibson. Darrell Evans. Jack Morris. But it was their 75-year-old manager who received the biggest ovation from the fans in Comerica Park.

"It was great to see Sparky so excited," Gibson said. "That was the one thing that struck us all."

Typical of his shyness, during his 2006 World Series visit, Anderson refused manager Jim Leyland's invitation to visit the clubhouse. But typical of his showmanship, Anderson gave a rousing pregame news conference that reminded many sportswriters how much they missed him. A few highlights:

- On his career: "I managed 26 years and found out when I retired I didn't own the game. I thought I owned it when I was managing all those years. You can climb to the top of the mountain, get down on your knees and kiss the ground, because you'll never own that mountain. That mountain is only owned by one single person, and he'll never give it up. That's the way baseball is."

- On the popularity of baseball: "The commissioner needs a tremendous bouquet for what he's done. He stepped in there now, and they're drawing all over.... I got a kick out of them when they used to say baseball is dying, and football is No. 1. I hate to break the sad news to football, but nothing will ever take the place of baseball. When it goes bad, call me, because I won't be around, but I can be reached under the ground."

- On his life: "I was so lucky that I almost at times...feel ashamed that you could be that lucky, all the things that happened for me." ●

Sparky Anderson won the American League Manager of the Year Award twice while he was with the Tigers. His first came when the team won the World Series in 1984. The second award came in 1987 when the first-place Tigers finished with a record of 98-64.

MARY SCHROEDER/DFP

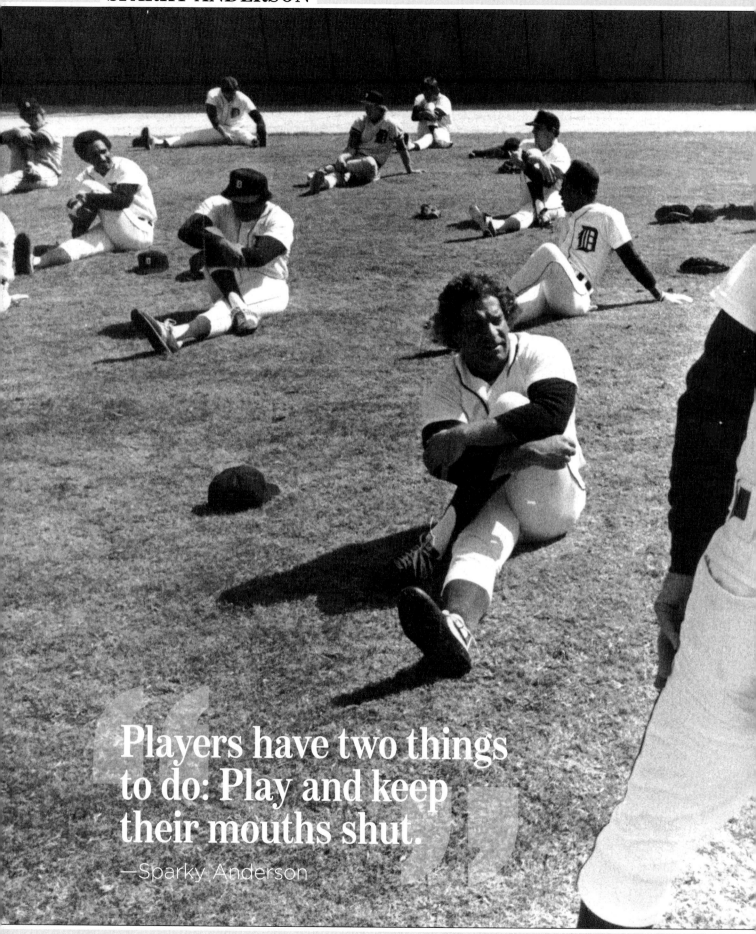

Players have two things
to do: Play and keep
their mouths shut.
—Sparky Anderson

Sparky Anderson's No. 11 has not yet been retired by the Detroit Tigers, but no one in the organization has worn that number since Sparky's retirement in 1995.

MARY SCHROEDER/DFP

SPARKY ANDERSON
TIMELINE

February 22, 1934:
Born in Bridgewater, South Dakota

1954:
Signed by Brooklyn Dodgers and went on to play five minor-league seasons with them.

December 23, 1958:
Traded by Brooklyn Dodgers to Philadelphia Phillies for three players, including outfielder Rip Repulski, and was installed as Phillies' regular second baseman for the following season.

April 10, 1959:
Made major league debut for Phillies.

July 19, 1959:
Had his first three-hit game in big leagues in 8-4 home loss to Dodgers. Exactly a week later, in a 6-3 win at Cincinnati, Anderson had his only other three-hit game.

September 27, 1959:
Played last big-league game. Finished only season with .218 average, no home runs and 34 RBI in 152 games for last-place Phillies.

1964:
Hired by Triple-A Toronto Maple Leafs owner Jack Kent Cooke (later majority owner of the Washington Redskins, Los Angeles Lakers and Los Angeles Kings) to manage for first time at age 30.

1965:
Won Western Carolinas League title with Rock Hill Cardinals.

1966: Lost in Florida State League finals with St. Petersburg Cardinals.

June 14, 1966: Anderson's St. Petersburg team lost 4–3 to Miami in 29 innings, still longest pro game played (by innings) without interruption.

1967: Lost in California League finals with Modesto Reds.

1968: Won Southern League title with Asheville Tourists.

1969: Served on coaching staff for expansion San Diego Padres.

1969-70: In off-season, accepted an offer to join Anaheim Angels coaching staff, but then was offered a chance to replace Dave Bristol as manager of Reds for 1970 season.

April 6, 1970:
Managed his first big-league game, a 5-1 Reds victory over Montreal. Reds would go on to win another 101 games but lost World Series in five games to Baltimore Orioles.

1972:
Led Reds to pennant again, but they lost to Oakland Athletics in World Series in seven games.

1973:
Led Reds to 99 wins and NL West title, but they lost to New York Mets 3-2 in NL Championship Series.

1975:
Led Reds to 108 wins and a classic, seven-game World Series title over Boston Red Sox.

1976:
Led Reds to 102 regular-season wins and a World Series sweep of New York Yankees.

1978:
Fired after back-to-back second-place finishes to the Dodgers because he refused to alter his coaching staff.

June 14, 1979:
Hired to manage Detroit Tigers. He made them a winner immediately but didn't get to the postseason until 1984.

1984:
Led Tigers to a 35-5 start en route to a 104-58 record—he was first manager to compile 100-win seasons in each league —and World Series title over San Diego. Anderson named American League Manager of the Year.

1987:
Led Tigers to a 98-64 record, best in majors, but they were upset by Minnesota Twins in ALCS. Anderson won his second AL Manager of the Year award.

1991:
Led Tigers to a second-place finish despite his team finishing last in batting average, first in batting strikeouts and near bottom in most pitching categories.

1995:
Resigned after a season in which he refused to manage replacement players at start of year, then returned when regular players did.

2000:
Inducted into Baseball Hall of Fame and Cincinnati Reds Hall of Fame.

May 28, 2005:
Jersey No. 10 was retired by Reds.

2006:
Construction was completed on George "Sparky" Anderson Field at Ullman Stadium at California Lutheran University's new athletic complex.

2007:
Inducted into Canadian Baseball Hall of Fame and Museum.

November 4, 2010:
Died in Thousand Oaks, California

By JOHN ERARDI
Cincinnati Enquirer

Reds Fans Mourn Skipper

Anderson cemented his legacy in Cincinnati by managing one of baseball's great dynasties

R eds fans will remember Sparky Anderson for three things: the way he was hired, the way he was fired, and everything in between. He was "Sparky Who?" in the headlines when he was hired as a 35-year-old, no-name manager at the end of the 1969 season. After his firing nine years later, he was mourned by fans throughout Reds Country as if they'd lost a loved one. In between, the "Main Spark" (a nickname he picked up from his pregame radio show) led the Reds to five divisional crowns, four World Series appearances and two World Championships.

Anderson died November 4 at his home in Thousand Oaks, Calif., of complications from dementia. He was 76.

"Knowing Sparky, he wouldn't have wanted one of his players to go first – he was always thinking of the other guy," said Pete Rose, whom Anderson named team captain on Oct. 9, 1969, the day Anderson got the Reds job. It was the second move Anderson made that day. The first was to name his first professional manager, George Scherger, his bench coach in Cincinnati, keeping a promise Anderson had made to "Sugar Bear" 17 years earlier.

"Today is a sad, sad day," said Tony Perez. "None of us wanted this

Sparky Anderson during spring training in 1974.

AP Images

"We all loved Sparky. He made all of us better.
—Tony Perez

Sparky Anderson and Pete Rose are one side of this engaging dugout conversation in Cincinnati.

day to come. We all loved Sparky. He made all of us better, made all of our lives better—not just as our manager, but as our friend and leader. He showed us the way, right up to the very end."

Anderson became just as famous—and every bit as colorful—as the great players he managed in Cincinnati: Rose, Perez, Johnny Bench and Joe Morgan, all Hall of Famers except Rose, who has been kept out by a gambling scandal.

"I was 35 years old when I went into Cincinnati in 1970," Anderson recalled a few years ago. "When I came out nine years later, the guys had made me a star. Over those nine years, they averaged 96 wins. I tell people, 'Just think what I could have done if I had some players!'"

And yet, for all of Anderson's self-deprecating humor, his plaque hangs in Cooperstown, N.Y., among his former players. Anderson was elected to the National Baseball Hall of Fame in 2000. On induction day that summer, he still couldn't believe it. "You look around, you say to yourself, 'My goodness...how could a young man from Bridgewater, South Dakota, 600 people, and couldn't ever be in front of a microphone, and they're talking about the third-winningest manager?'"

George Lee Anderson was born on Feb. 22, 1934, in Bridgewater, S.D. He played in the minor leagues for the Brooklyn Dodgers and made the major leagues as a starting second baseman for the Philadelphia Phillies in 1959.

His playing career was forgettable except for one thing: That's where he obtained the nickname "Sparky." As Anderson described it in his 1990 book *Sparky*, he spent more time as a young player arguing with umpires than making plays on the bases.

"There was an old radio announcer whose name I don't remember. 'The sparks are flying tonight,' he'd say after I charged another umpire. Then I'd do it the next night. And the next. Finally he got to saying, 'And here comes Sparky racing toward the umpire again.' The

Sparky posing with Sparky: Anderson visited the Reds Hall of Fame Museum in 2004 to see the bronzed image of himself honoring his time in Cincinnati.

STAFF PHOTOGRAPHER/CE

> " **You give us the pitching some of these clubs have, and no one could touch us, but God has a way of not arranging that because it's not as much fun.** "
>
> —Sparky Anderson

Even though Sparky was known to have a few heated debates with umpires around the league, he was only ejected 47 times in his 26 seasons as a manager.

name stuck. At first, I was embarrassed. Eventually, I got used to it."

After he stopped playing, Anderson began coaching. He was a manager in the minor leagues for five years, then was hired as a coach in 1969 with the San Diego Padres. A year later, he was managing the Reds.

If there is a sportswriter who didn't love Anderson for his ease with a good quote, his genuine warmth for people and deep love of the game, that scribe has never revealed it. Anderson would give the first wave of reporters to his pre-game office one set of quotes, and then make up an entirely new batch for the second wave.

One writer recalled Anderson talking away in his office right up to game time. "Excuse me," Anderson finally said. "They're about to play the national anthem."

Anderson never gave the impression that he regarded himself as anything but the luckiest man on the face of the earth.

His position players adored him—some of his starting pitchers had other adjectives to describe him—and typical of those who adored him was Rose, whom Anderson named captain upon getting the managerial job in Cincinnati. "I'd walk through hell in a gasoline suit for Sparky," Rose would go on to say, more than once.

Anderson, whose nicknames also included "Captain Hook," thanks to his penchant for removing any starting pitcher showing even the least sign of struggling, was a bigger-than-life character who never acted like it. He was part Casey Stengel (non-sequiturs), part John McGraw (terrific in-game tactician) and part Connie Mack (statesman of the game). In the pantheon, Anderson ranks right up there with all of them.

At the time of his retirement from baseball in 1995, Anderson's 2,194 victories were third in baseball history, behind only Mack and McGraw. Until 2006, when Tony La Russa matched the feat, Anderson was the only manager to have won world championships in both leagues.

Cincinnati fans will mourn the loss of one of the greatest managers in their team's proud history.

Sparky celebrates his first National League pennant in 1970, Anderson's first season as a major league manager.

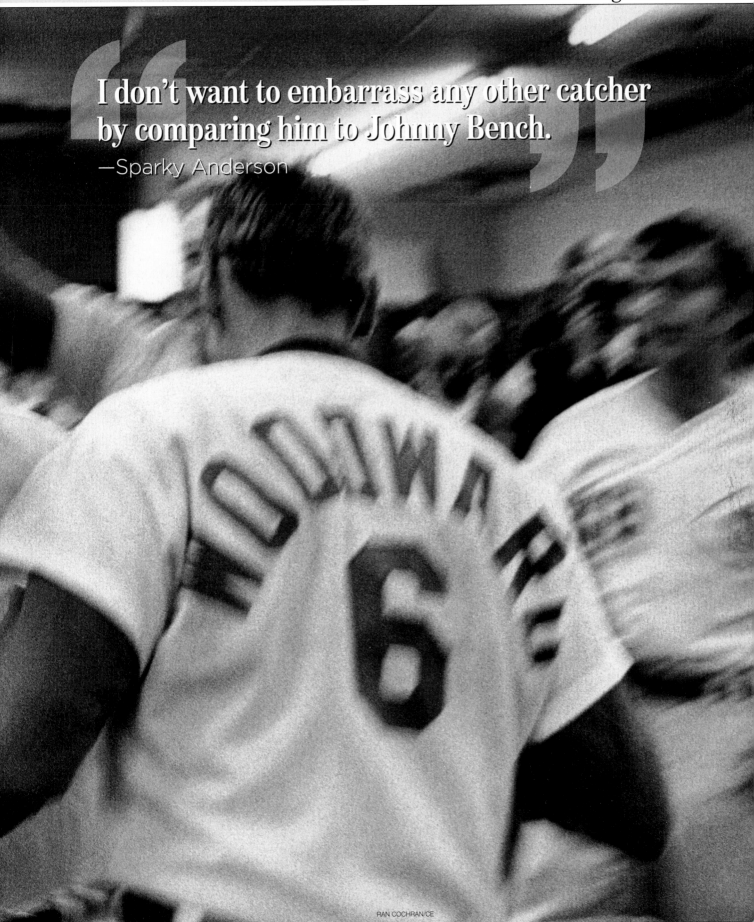

"I don't want to embarrass any other catcher by comparing him to Johnny Bench."
—Sparky Anderson

La Russa, who won titles with the Oakland Athletics and St. Louis Cardinals, later said he thought Anderson shouldn't have to share that achievement. "I said it once and I'll say it again," La Russa told *The New York Times* in 2006. "I have such a respect and affection for Sparky that I believe he's one of the greatest—not just managers—but baseball men and ambassadors for the game. It's such a great honor, he should really have this alone."

Anderson managed the Detroit Tigers to the 1984 World Series championship. He was the team's manager from mid-1979 to 1995. Those 17 seasons at the helm were the most in Tigers history.

And yet when it came time to go into the National Baseball Hall of Fame, there never seemed to be any doubt in Anderson's mind which cap he would wear. On the day his beloved friend, former Reds general manager Bob Howsam, died on Feb. 19, 2008, Sparky explained why Cincinnati would always be No. 1 to him.

"People (in Detroit) said, 'Why wear a Reds cap? Why not a Tigers cap? You were in Detroit for 17 years.' I said, 'Because of Bob Howsam. Without Bob Howsam, I don't ever get to Detroit,'" he said.

At the time Howsam hired him, Anderson had never managed above the Triple-A level. Their relationship was marked by mutual respect and trust. Anderson wasn't afraid to make controversial decisions, and none raised more eyebrows than his decision to move Pete Rose to third base in 1975.

Howsam was out of town at the time, and while Anderson didn't have to secure anybody's permission to move Rose to third, he did tell a few people. Reds broadcaster Marty Brennaman didn't believe it until he saw it, and he says he'll never forget Rose's first chance.

"The first batter up—Ralph Garr—hit an absolute screamer to Pete's glove side. Pete breaks to his left, stumbles, fields the ball, recovers and gets up and throws him out. He looked like a monkey playing with a football. It was incredible."

Sparky Anderson addresses the crowd at Riverfront Stadium before opening day in 1976.

The next day Howsam called Chief Bender, the Reds director of player personnel. "I looked at the paper this morning," began Howsam, "and the box score said 'Pete Rose—third base.' That's a mistake, right?"

"No, Bob. Sparky put him at third base."

"Oh, my God," said Howsam.

The Reds went on to win the World Series that season and would repeat in 1976. Two years later, following two second-place finishes in their division, the Reds fired Anderson after he refused to replace any of his coaches.

"I've seen people write and say, 'Bob Howsam fired you,'" recalled Anderson. "Or 'Dick Wagner (Howsam's No. 2 man) fired you.' No, they didn't. I fired myself. I was told to let three of my coaches go, and I wouldn't do it. I'd brought them in, and I wasn't going to take them out. They had no choice but to fire me. I wouldn't do what they wanted."

It wasn't the first time Anderson hadn't done what they wanted. It was just the first time he got fired for it.

"People know what they have here," said Anderson during a memorable final farewell in 2002 to Riverfront Stadium, dubbed by former Reds beat writer Bob Hertzel in the Big Red Machine years as "The Land of Ahs."

"I say it all the time," began Anderson. "If you've never played in Cincinnati, you've never played. And when I say Cincinnati, we're actually saying all the way down to Louisville, and over to Portsmouth and up to Columbus: Reds Country."

And to the end, Sparky Anderson was its king. ●

Following his death, Cincinnati fans honored Sparky outside the Great American Ball Park by placing memorabilia and other tokens of appreciation in memory of their great manager of the 1970s.

By PAUL DAUGHERTY
Cincinnati Enquirer

Thanks for the Memories

If a nickname ever aptly described a person,
it was George Lee Anderson's

If sports provide the carnival music of our lives, Sparky Anderson was the barker. It was a good time to be alive and in Cincinnati in the 1970s. You could thank Sparky for some of that. Leaning forward from the dugout rail, yapping at his "boys," loving baseball and his role in it. A lucky man who knew it.

Not long ago, he stopped eating. Dementia does that to a person. Swallowing can be impaired; the connection between eating and staying alive is lost. It's as if the brain tells the body "enough."

He died peacefully and without fanfare Thursday. George Lee Anderson was 76. There's some wonderful and ironic Big Red symmetry there.

Dying peacefully wasn't especially like Sparky Anderson. He was gregarious, loving and well-loved. The no-fanfare would have been OK with him, though. He'd have appreciated that. Sparky wouldn't want no fuss made.

"It's them guys out there that do it," he might say, stretching a finger in the direction of the ballfield. "It wasn't what I did. It was what they did. I got the easiest job in the world."

He managed the Reds to four pennants and two world titles. He arrived in 1970, a 36-year-old career bus rider that Lee May referred

When Sparky was named the manager of the Reds in 1969, the headlines read "Sparky Who?" When he left town in 1979 he was one of the best-known sports personalities in Cincinnati history.

STAFF PHOTOGRAPHER/CE

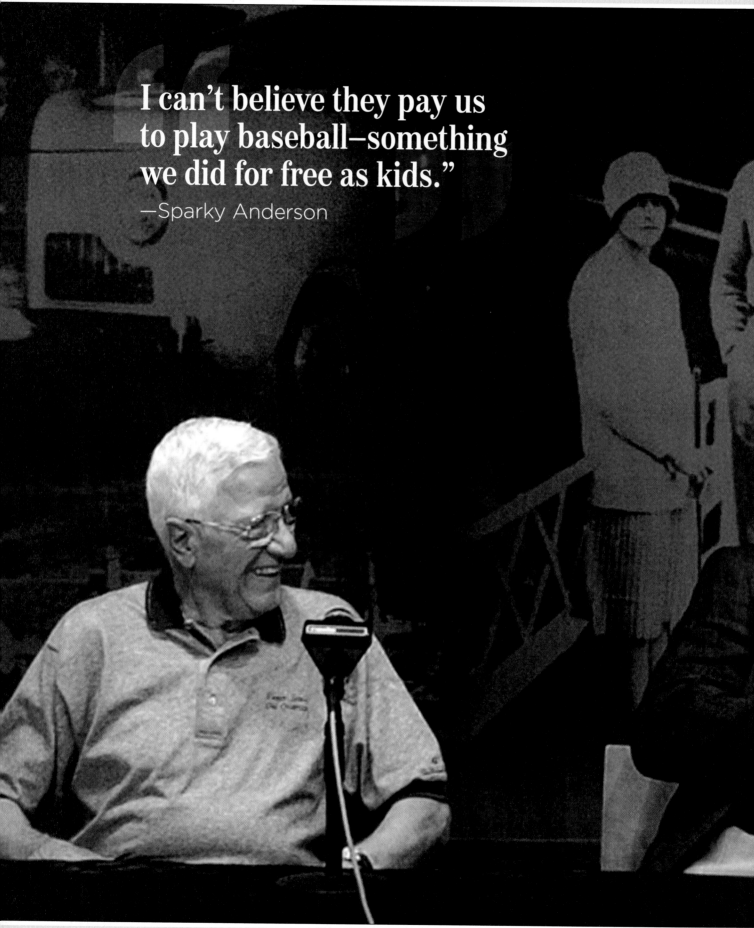

"I can't believe they pay us to play baseball–something we did for free as kids."

—Sparky Anderson

Alex Grammas looks on as Johnny Bench and Sparky Anderson joke around during the press conference before the Cincinnati Reds retire his No. 10 jersey in May of 2005.

MEGGAN BOOKER/CE

to early on as "that minor-league mother." He departed nine years later as the jockey who rode the Secretariat of major league teams.

Anderson was comfortable with fame. It just never changed him, which was remarkable. He was also easy with crediting everyone else, a trait that served the Reds well during their star-filled run. "He had everyone's respect, but he had to earn it, and he did," Johnny Bench recalled Wednesday.

A few years ago, I did a book with Bench. We talked at length about Sparky. Bench said the Main Spark's best attribute was his ability to manage people. From the book, *Catch Every Ball*:

"Sparky took the time to know his players individually, so when he needed to motivate someone, he knew what made him tick.

Anderson would consult The Big Four (Bench, Pete Rose, Tony Perez, Joe Morgan) before recommending a trade to the general manager. If we didn't like the player or didn't believe he'd fit our team, we'd veto him. If there was a guy available we wouldn't like to have dinner with, he wouldn't be on our club.

Joe, Pete, Tony and I ruled the clubhouse. One spring, Sparky told the team, "I have one set of rules for you guys, and one set for them," pointing to The Big Four. "Their rules are, they have no rules."

"He relied on our information, but made the decisions," said Bench. "And 99.9 percent of the time, he was right."

The Big Four repaid Anderson's respect for them with championships, and love of the sort only ballplayers know. Pete Rose visited Anderson recently; Bench and Morgan saw him in August, in Cooperstown at the Hall of Fame induction ceremonies. "It was sad," Bench recalled.

Anderson couldn't hear. He'd gotten new hearing aids not long before he made the trip to Cooperstown, but had forgotten to remove them when he took a shower. "When you can't hear, it's like you're living in a vacuum. His social life stopped," Bench said. "We were just all holding our breath in Cooperstown, hoping he'd make a comeback."

Bench recalled a photo he took of his former manager that day. "He had a faraway look in his eyes," Bench said, "like he was already gone."

I asked Bench to look into his mind's eye and fetch an image of Anderson.

"Smiling, happy and brilliant," Bench said. "That lean he always had…. The fact he never stepped on a foul line…'Big John, how ya doin'?'…we're in spring training once, in the outfield doing calisthenics. He came up, started feinting, like he was boxing. I clipped him with a left jab on top of his head. He wanted to be one of the guys.

"Sparky gave me stature," Bench continued. "He gave the team a level of professionalism and the fans a team that would be respected."

Icons die ingloriously, same as the rest of us. The difference is the memories they bequeath.

Once upon a time, there was a team that played baseball as well as any before or since. Sparky Anderson managed it. We all were younger then. ●

Sparky's major league managerial career started at the young age of 36 when the Cincinnati Reds General Manager Bob Howsam gave him a chance at the job.

"**Baseball is a simple game. If you have good players and if you keep them in the right frame of mind, then the manager is a success.**"

—Sparky Anderson

JEFF SWINGER/CE

Reds manager Dave Miley listens to some words of advice from Sparky Anderson on May 28, 2005. Sparky was being honored before the game by having his number retired by the Cincinnati Reds.

STAFF REPORT
Cincinnati Enquirer

The Man Behind the Fungo

Sparky's baseball success is well documented, but here are things you might not know

In 1953, George Lee Anderson began his minor-league career in Class C ball at Santa Barbara, Calif., in the Brooklyn Dodgers organization. He had played three seasons of varsity baseball at Dorsey High School in Los Angeles. His future Reds bench coach, George Scherger, was Santa Barbara's second baseman and player-manager, 13 years Anderson's senior.

Anderson was fearless, Scherger recalled a few years ago, noting how the youngster would kneel in front of the base on tag plays at second and throw himself around the bases with abandon.

Anderson progressed up the Dodgers chain. At Class Double-A Fort Worth in the Texas League in 1955, a radio announcer hung the nickname "Sparky" on him for his feisty play, and it stuck.

He made it to the big leagues with Philadelphia for one season, in 1959, but did his best work with the bat at Triple-A Montreal three years earlier.

When managing the Reds, Sparky Anderson had great respect for Johnny Bench as a player and a person. This is proven by how good of friends the two remained after Anderson's time in Cincinnati.

"I had 81 hits in my first 167 at-bats," Anderson recalled in 1997. "I was hitting .485. Believe it or not, I beat out 16 push-bunts.... People couldn't believe it. No one could hit .485 with a stroke like that. But everything I hit fell in."

The hands-in-pockets arguing

Anderson's habit of keeping his hands in his back pockets while disputing calls stemmed from the time he tried to throw an umpire to the ground in Rock Hill, S.C., while managing the St. Louis Cardinals' Class D team in 1965.

"I was very hot-tempered, used to really get into it," Anderson once said. "I go out onto the field and start arguing with the ump, and he bumps me.... He didn't mean to do it. It was an accident. But I was so wound up, I grabbed him with both my hands up around his chest and tried to throw him to the ground. They tore me off of him and got me inside the locker room.

"I knew I was done. Done for at least the rest of the year, and maybe done for good.... So I'm sittin' there, feelin' bad.

"I look up. It's the umpire. 'Sparky, can we talk?' I said, 'Oh gosh, yes.' I didn't know what he was gonna say or do. He said, 'You know, I didn't mean to bump you. And I won't deny that I did. But here's what we're gonna do. You got run for bad language. That's the truth of it, and that's how I'm going to report it. Everything else came after I bumped you. You don't deserve a long suspension, and I'm going to report it in such a way that you don't get one.'

"I never forgot it. That man, in his own way, saved my career.... From that day forward, I started putting my hands in my back pockets."

His firing by the Reds

Anderson was fired after the 1978 season after consecutive second-place finishes. It was rumored that assistant general manager Dick Wagner was behind it. Others believed GM Bob Howsam pulled the trigger.

But the Reds weren't ones to air their dirty laundry in public, and Anderson had too much class to blame anybody, given that the organization had given him his big chance to manage in the major leagues in 1970.

When Howsam died in 2008, Anderson finally said what really had happened.

"I fired myself," he said. "I was told to let three of my coaches go, and I wouldn't do it. I'd brought them in, and I wasn't going to take them out. They had no choice but to fire me. I wouldn't do what they wanted."

Anderson said he held no grudges over the firing.

"Bob let me hire all my coaches (in 1970)," Anderson said. "Thirty-five years old, just a nobody, allowed to hire my own coaches. He said, 'The only stipulation I have is that when you bring me the list, if there's somebody I don't like, that you'll remove him.' There wasn't a single person on that list I wasn't allowed to hire. Bob was a person of trust."

You couldn't tell it by this picture, but Sparky could have a fiery temper when on the field. An altercation with an umpire during his minor league years prompted Sparky to keep his hands in his back pockets when arguing a call with an umpire.

CARRIE COCHRAN/CE

The jersey numbers

The Reds retired Sparky Anderson's No. 10 in 2005 but the Detroit Tigers—whom Anderson led to 1,331 victories over 17 seasons to become their winningest manager ever—never retired his No. 11.

When the Tigers recognized the 25th anniversary of the 1984 World Series champion team in 2009, *Detroit News* columnist Tom Gage implored the club to use the occasion to recognize Anderson.

"What on earth is preventing you?" Gage wrote. "The Cincinnati Reds have retired it. The Fort Worth Kats have retired it."

It has been speculated a falling out with owner Mike Ilitch over Anderson's refusal to manage replacement players in 1995 had something to do with the stance.

The legendary battle in 1984

In 1984 Anderson became the first manager in major league history to win World Series while leading clubs in both leagues (Tony La Russa became the second in 2006), but it's interesting to note that the record was a foregone conclusion that season.

The only thing to be decided was who would get it.

The manager in the other dugout, San Diego's Dick Williams, had won World Series in 1972 and 1973 with the Oakland Athletics.

The second firing in Cincinnati

Anderson guest-starred as himself on an episode of *WKRP in Cincinnati* that ran in 1979. The episode was titled "Sparky," and the plot had Anderson hired to host a sports interview show at the radio station. Alas, it doesn't go well and the show eventually fails, prompting Anderson to say, "Every time I come into this town, I get fired." ●

Cincinnati catcher Jason LaRue congratulates Sparky Anderson with a pat on the back after his number retirement ceremony at Great American Ball Park in 2005.

By JOHN ERARDI
Cincinnati Enquirer

The Nicest Man in Sports

Sparky Anderson had love for just about eveyone he encountered

Somebody once asked Sparky Anderson what was his favorite kind of music. "The love songs," he answered. No three words ever described a man better. In 25 years of covering sports in Cincinnati, I only once got somebody's autograph—Sparky Anderson's.

Under the strictures of the Baseball Writers Association of America, I wasn't supposed to get any. I made a one-time exception for my mother, bedridden from multiple sclerosis. Sparky was one of her favorite guys, so I figured what the heck.

Besides, it wasn't a public setting; it was just me and Sparky. I recall it taking place in Louisville in the mid-to-late 1980s when Anderson's Detroit Tigers were in town to play an exhibition game.

I think we talked about Sparky's and my mother's love of country music. I've never been a big fan of the genre, but I understood their point: Country-and-western songs have the best storylines.

I remember leaving our meeting thinking, "Man, what a nice guy."

I've never had a feeling on the job quite like that since—except when I'd see Sparky again.

I'm writing this not because Sparky has just died. I've been saying

With Johnny Bench over his right shoulder, Sparky Anderson blows a kiss to the fans at Great American Ball Park.

JEFF SWINGER/CE

> "If I ever find a pitcher who has heat, a good curve and a slider, I might seriously consider marrying him, or at least proposing."
>
> —Sparky Anderson

> "The only reason I'm coming out here tomorrow is because the schedule says I have to."
>
> —Sparky Anderson

After Sparky was fired as Reds manager in 1978 and before he was hired to manage the Detroit Tigers in June 1979 he took a job as a television commentator. Here Sparky interviews his successor in Cincinnati, manager John McNamara.

FRED STRAUB/CE

it for years whenever somebody has asked me who is the nicest person I've ever met in sports. My answer's always been the same: "Sparky Anderson—nobody else even close."

Everybody who ever met Sparky has a Sparky story, because he was congenitally kind. Sparky would dispute the congenital part. He says he learned it from his father growing up in Bridgewater, S.D.

It doesn't cost anything to be nice to people.

My *Enquirer* colleague Bill Koch recently told me of having driven with another journalist to the Otesaga Hotel in Cooperstown, N.Y., late in the afternoon on the day of their arrival for Induction Weekend at the Baseball Hall of Fame. They were scrambling for a first-day story, as often happens for journalists.

They found a side road onto which to pull their rental car. As they approached the hotel, who should be walking down the driveway and headed back to the hotel? "Hey, Lonnie, check this out," Koch pointed.

It was none other than George "Sparky" Anderson, media gold, dropped down from heaven.

"He didn't know me," Koch said. "He didn't have to stop and talk. But he stood there and talked to us for 30 minutes like we were his next-door neighbors."

Which, of course, was the charm of the man.

I didn't know Sparky well, but he always gave me a smile and handshake that I took to mean he remembered my face.

How sweet that twinkle of recognition.

I remember once being in the manager's office in Detroit where I had gone to write a feature on the Tigers manager.

I lost track of the time. It was Sparky who woke me from my reverie.

"Excuse me—that's the national anthem," he said. "I'm always out there for the anthem."

It was 10 minutes before game time. I should have out of his office a half hour earlier. We'd been talking about the Big Red

Sparky Anderson points out Reds great Tony Perez during his number retirement ceremony in 2005.

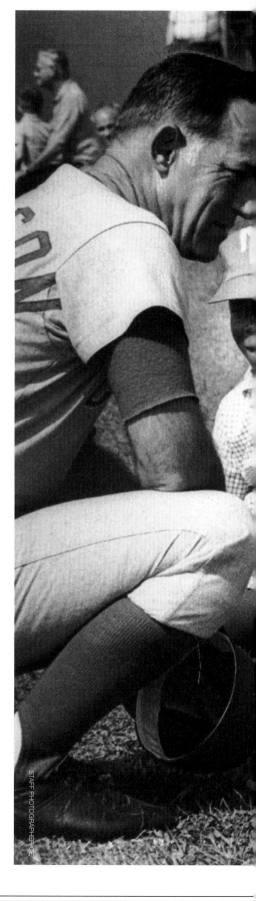

Machine; he could've gone on forever. Not because he needed to, but because I needed him to.

There is only one other person I've ever met who was so totally devoid of any pretense whatsoever about his celebrity: Joe Nuxhall.

Toward the end of Sparky's 17-year run in Detroit, I recall hearing that he had to take a leave of absence; he was exhausted. There was, we were told, a public and a private Anderson. "Sparky" never said no to anybody when he was managing, on the field or off. Back home in Thousand Oaks, "George" Anderson could say no.

But it wasn't a phony "Sparky." It couldn't have been. Nobody can be that nice that long unless it's real. Besides, there are countless stories of him back home in the neighborhood, being everybody's best friend, even when he was just out taking a walk.

Before I got into sports writing, I was driving to work one day in the mid-1970s, and who should cross the street in front of me—between downtown and Riverfront Stadium—but Sparky Anderson. I'd never before seen the man except from the stands or on TV. He was carrying his dry-cleaning. It caught me off-guard. It shouldn't have. It was Sparky. He picked up and dropped off his own laundry. I would later learn that Sparky was a "neat freak."

That day, a couple of horns of recognition honked. I remember yelling something at the Reds' skipper—he was God in this town in the mid-1970s—something like, "Hey, Main Spark!" He waved back.

That's the way I'll remember him.

I've never written a story about somebody without saying something more than "What a nice guy." I don't expect I ever will again.

Sparky Anderson was one of a kind. ●

The April after winning his first World Series Championship with the Cincinnati Reds, Sparky takes time to talk to some Little Leaguers about what else—baseball.

STAFF REPORT
Cincinnati Enquirer

Sparky Recollections

Fond memories from those who knew him

Tony Perez

Big Red Machine first baseman, Hall of Famer.

"He'd call me in and say, 'Things aren't right in the clubhouse. You got to say something to so-and-so.' Whenever something wasn't right in the clubhouse, it was my fault! But that's the relationship we had. He'd have other guys say things for him, too—Pete, Joe, Johnny—but for some reason it was 'my' clubhouse. He knew I could say something without somebody taking it personally, but still get the message across."

In 1970, Anderson's first year on the job, Lee May, Perez's close friend and a clubhouse cutup, good-naturedly called Anderson—who had played only one year in the majors and done all his managing down on the farms—a "minor-league (expletive deleted)." That "expletive" was baseball's $64,000 multipurpose pejorative.

"I can't remember where it was—the bus, the plane, somewhere like that," Perez recalls. "We'd had a few drinks. Everybody laughed, but afterward Sparky called me in. He said, 'Take care of your buddy.' And I did. Yeah, Lee got me in trouble with that one, but I took care of it. That's the way Sparky was. He could take a jab, but if he thought somebody had crossed the line, he'd tell me to take care of it. And I would."

—John Erardi

STAFF PHOTOGRAPHER/CE

This is one of Sparky's calmer moments conversing on the field with the umpires in his early days with the Reds.

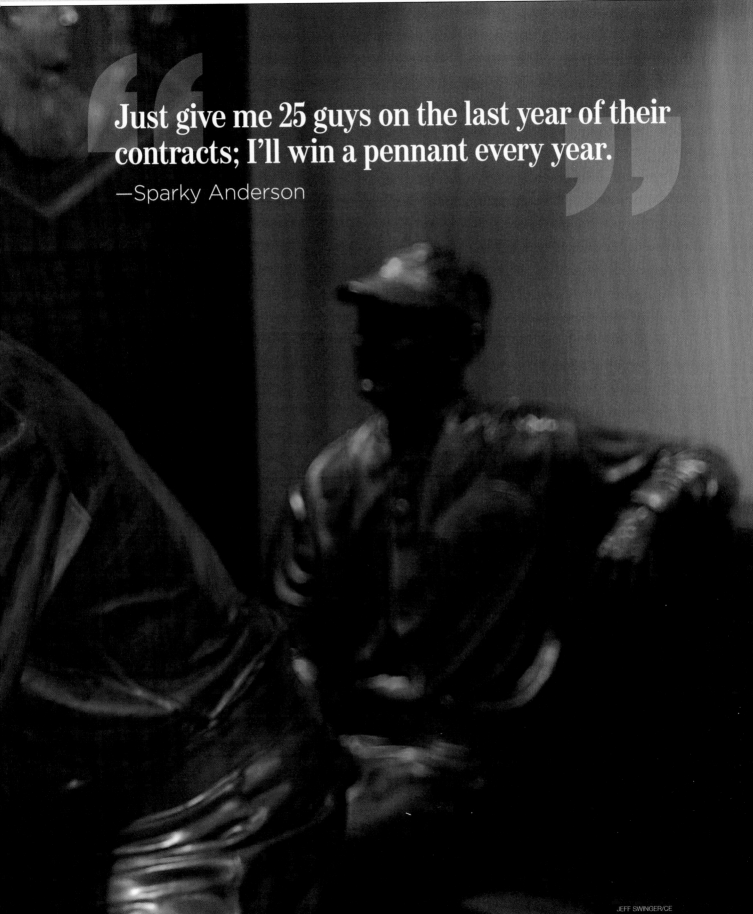

"Just give me 25 guys on the last year of their contracts; I'll win a pennant every year.

—Sparky Anderson

JEFF SWINGER/CE

Hal McCoy

Hall of Fame baseball writer, covered Anderson for the **Dayton Daily News** *during the Big Red Machine era.*

"Before the first game of the 1975 World Series, I was in his office with the first wave of writers," McCoy said. "Someone asked him this one question, and Sparky answered it in his usual, informative way. Those writers left, and I stayed as the next wave came in. Another writer wound up asking Sparky the exact same question he had answered in the first wave, and Sparky answered it the exact opposite way.

"That wave leaves, and I asked Sparky why he had given two different answers. He said, 'Well, you can't give every writer the same story.' That's how accommodating he was. He wanted to give everybody something to write about."

—Tom Groeschen

Walt Terrell

St. Henry baseball coach played for Anderson twice in Detroit, from 1985-88 and 1990-92.

"I can't believe he had me twice; what a lack of judgment on his part," Terrell joked—and they shared a keen sense of humor. They also shared quite a few moments on the pitcher's mound.

"When he took you out, you weren't allowed to say anything. You had to put the ball in his hand softly and walk quietly off the field. That was the rule.... I remember one time in the eighth inning and I had given up four runs or so when he came out to get me. He took two or three steps onto the field and I said, 'What took you so long?' And he said, 'I was in the bathroom. I didn't know you were getting beat up this bad.'"

—Ryan Ernst

During spring training in 1979 Sparky Anderson was in Reds camp as a television commentator interviewing players and coaches. It was a big change from what he was doing with the Reds during spring training in 1978.

Bob Hertzel

Enquirer *beat writer during the Big Red Machine days.*

"The mail arrived in the department in the morning, but the reporters didn't start to tumble in until mid-afternoon. It was the time of year when the Christmas cards would come in, this being in the days before computers, where cards were actually made of paper and were hand-signed. One that arrived that afternoon in December 1970 had us all stumped though, for it carried warm Christmas greetings from George Anderson.

"George Anderson? Who is George Anderson, we all thought. You know a George Anderson? No? We mused over the matter for about 30 minutes and couldn't place him.

"Then, all of a sudden, someone said, 'Hey, what's Sparky's first name?' And there it was. Sparky Anderson, the manager of the Reds, the man who had won a pennant and 70 of his first 100 games as a major league manager, had sent the local sports department a Christmas card under his given name."

—Tom Groeschen

STAFF PHOTOGRAPHER/CE

Sparky loved to play the game of baseball, he just wasn't good enough to make a career of it. He would routinely grab a glove before a game in his earlier days and join the team on the infield.

STAFF REPORT
Cincinnati Enquirer

Baseball's Loss

Reaction from Major League Baseball to the death of Sparky Anderson

"You never heard a bad word ever about Sparky. He was a good man. He did a lot of great things."
—All-Star player and manager Don Zimmer

"All of baseball mourns the passing of one of the game's all-time great managers and ambassadors. In one way or another, Sparky touched the life of every Reds fan."
—Reds CEO Bob Castellini

"He was a big part of my life, for sure. He had a lot to do with molding me professionally and taught me a lot about perseverance. He was a good guy. Baseball will have very few people like Sparky. He was a unique individual. He was a character with a great passion and love for the game."
—Former Tigers pitcher Jack Morris

STAFF PHOTOGRAPHER/CE

Sparky strays from his signature stance of keeping his hands in his back pockets when arguing with an umpire.

"I think he was a great manager because he was a great handler of people. He had great players with the Big Red Machine, but he didn't always have the greatest teams in Detroit when I was around him a lot. But he had a knack for getting the best out of people. He knew when to pat them on the back and when to kick them in the butt. That's the ultimate manager, I think."
—Umpire Tim McClelland

"I recall with great fondness the many hours we would spend together when his Tigers came to Milwaukee. Sparky was a loyal friend, and whenever I would be dealing with difficult situations as commissioner, he would lift my spirits, telling me to keep my head up and that I was doing the right thing."
—MLB commissioner Bud Selig

"Sparky was one of the greatest people I've met in baseball. He was a leader to his players both on and off the field. He was an incredible person, and I cherish the time I was able to spend with him."
—Tigers Hall of Famer Al Kaline

"With Sparky, even if everyone didn't get along off the field, by God, they were all together when they were on it."
—Former Red Tommy Helms

Joe Morgan tries to help Sparky explain how he saw the play to the umpire during a game at Riverfront Stadium.

STAFF PHOTOGRAPHER/CE

"
My idea of managing is giving the ball to Tom Seaver and sitting down and watching him work.

—Sparky Anderson

"
I only had a high school education, and believe me, I had to cheat to get that.

—Sparky Anderson

Even fans who were too young to remember or know Sparky Anderson as the manager of the Cincinnati Reds paid homage to him during his number retirement ceremony in 2005.

JEFF SWINGER/CE

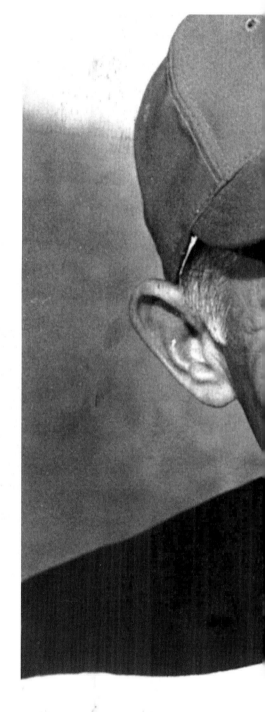

"Sparky was a heck of a manager and handled personalities on the team very well. ... He was like a father to the guys on the team."
—Former Red Gary Nolan

"He loved young players, and I respected the heck out of him. He always was upbeat and positive, friendly to everyone he ever met."
—Former Red Ron Oester

"Baseball has lost one of its great members. ... He represented the game to the highest degree of class, dignity and character."
—Hall of Fame manager Tommy Lasorda

"That last time I saw him was a couple years ago in Cooperstown. We had dinner at the same table. Just a wonderful man, a great baseball man. He was one of the most positive, upbeat guys I've ever met."
—Reds GM Walt Jocketty

"Not only did his jovial disposition, warm demeanor, infectious smile and innate ability to build confidence allow him to get the most out of his players, but it assured him of befriending everyone he touched. He will be missed in Cooperstown, especially during Hall of Fame Weekend, where he was a favorite among the fans and his fellow Hall of Famers."
—National Baseball Hall of Fame president Jeff Idelson

Sparky Anderson was always proud to slap on the ball cap and put on the jersey to go out and manage.

Cincinnati Fans
REMEMBER

SPARKY WAS a tremendous motivator, and really had a keen sense for managing difficult ego types on the team. I didn't know him personally, but I sure wish that I had. I hope that he's in glory right now.
—Bill Wilson, Loveland, Ohio

OUTSIDE OF JOE Nuxhall I do not think there was a more beloved Cincinnati Red. He was "Sparky Who?" when he was hired here in 1970. But his tenure in Cincinnati produced five playoff teams, four World Series and two World Champions. That was the Big Red Machine and he was the driver. Sparky was an entertaining speaker at local sports stags and a person always willing to sign autographs. He was one of a kind and will be missed by local baseball fans. It should be noted that the Reds Big Red Machine came to an abrupt end upon his departure in 1978.

—Tino D. Thomas, White Oak, Ohio

SPARKY WILL go down in history as the greatest manager the Cincinnati Reds have ever had in the dugout. He took the Reds the final step to winning the series, and doing it back-to-back years was totally awesome for me and all the Big Red Machine fans of the 1970s.

I will never forget one day at Riverfront when I helped a child retrieve a ball close to the wall down the third base line, lowering him over the fence by his legs to get the ball. Sparky gave us a big wave and a thumbs up for our effort.

Some of the best times of my life were spent at Riverfront watching my Reds play and battle the Dodgers year in and year out, and Sparky was as valuable as any player on the roster. Sparky will be missed by his family and friends, but also by so many baseball fans.

—Mike Whaley, Midway, Kentucky

ALTHOUGH SPARKY Anderson couldn't string two grammatically correct sentences together, he had as much class in his little finger as Audrey Hepburn had in her entire lineage. Remember, "There ain't no English teachers living in Indian Hill." God bless you, Sparky.

—T.J. Hughes Jr., Blue Ash, Ohio

Online comments:

GOD BLESS YOU, Sparky. I hope the Old Lefthander was one of the first ones there to welcome you.
—Redsfansince67

IT'S WITH A HEAVY heart that I say rest in peace to one of my childhood heroes. A gentleman and friend to everyone he ever met, including me. God speed to the "Main Spark," and comfort to his friends and family.
—Factcity

BESIDES BEING one of the greatest managers in baseball history, Sparky Anderson is one of the nicest gentlemen I have met in my life. He came to Charleston, West Virginia, in 1995 to speak to our local bar association and his speech was not so much about baseball, but more about his philosophy of life. He explained how his father raised him to always be kind to everyone he meets. Growing up in the 1970s, none of us knew how blessed we were to see the great players and this super human being who managed them. What a treasure to have witnessed what we did.
—Mark5760

GOD BLESS YOU, Sparky. Thank you for the memories! The Lord must have needed a man to manage his Angels. He just brought home the best.
—Bearcatvol

REST IN PEACE, Sparky. People often ask me what I love/loved about growing up and living in Cin-city and the first answer to my lips was always THE REDS! A job well done, as a manager and a MAN!
—Cincykidwest

A TRULY GREAT MAN, on and off the field. I hope the Reds do the right thing and create a permanent remembrance of Sparky within the organization.
—Theayatollah

SPARKY, THANK YOU for the memories! I loved watching the Big Red Machine as a child. I pray you're managing in a better place.
—Dartagnan

HEAVEN JUST got themselves one heckuva good manager. RIP, Captain Hook.
—Cabrillo

THE FORCE THAT turned the wheels of the Big Red Machine, Sparky was a credit to the great game of baseball. I am deeply saddened at his passing. My deepest sympathy to his family.

—Bev Levine, Kenwood, Ohio

By MITCH ALBOM
Detroit Free Press
First published: Monday, Oct. 2, 1995

Sparky's Last Game

Though Sparky was beloved by fans inside and outside Detroit, his team's losing record at the end of his career tore him up inside

He arrived for his last game hours before the first pitch, early Sunday morning, as the fog was breaking up and most people were still in church. He removed his clothes in stages, hanging up his gray sports coat, followed by the tie and the shoes. He pulled his baseball shirt over his dark slacks and socks, and he sat down that way, half-man, half-manager, munching a doughnut and holding the omnipresent cup of black coffee, part of the reason his hands now tremble like a nervous safecracker.

The other reason is that he is 61 years old.

"Here's something I don't get," he said, his voice almost as craggy as his leathered face. "We've been losing for years, and I get treated like a king. One night, we were leaving the park, and a guy yelled, 'Sparky, you're a legend!' And I said, 'Does a legend lose this many games?'

"And you know what? The guy didn't care."

Anderson shook his head. He cares. He is sick of losing. He is sick of going back to the hotel room and looking at his lineup and knowing that tomorrow he probably will lose again, and next year won't be any better than last year. He no longer loves the men he works for, and without that, Sparky Anderson, in his mind, owes you nothing.

Sparky Anderson managed his final game on October 1, 1995, as the Detroit Tigers wrapped up the season against the Baltimore Orioles at Camden Yards in Baltimore.

AP IMAGES

So this morning, he will announce his departure from the Tigers, after 17 years. It is not a retirement, not a firing. In typical Sparky fashion, everyone is a little confused.

And few people realize what they're about to lose.

There goes ol' Silver Hair. The best manager the Detroit Tigers ever had has danced around the subject of his departure all year, but he talked about it Sunday: "It's time to go. Let them get someone new in here, some new blood, give them a new kick, get them back in a war."

"And you?" he was asked.

He looked at his feet, still tucked inside the white rubber shower slippers that, for one more day, bore his No. 11.

"I'll tell you this. I'm not calling no teams. I'm not contacting no teams. If nobody calls me, I will not be offended."

He leaned back in his chair. They'll call, and he knows it.

There goes ol' Silver Hair.

• • • • • • • • • • • • • • •

The phone rang. It had been ringing all morning, friends wishing him luck, friends asking him questions, where will he go, what will he do? This time it was Jim Campbell, the man who brought Sparky to Detroit in 1979.

After Sparky says good-bye to the current ownership today, he will have lunch with Campbell and the longtime team physician, Clarence Livingood, before getting on a plane and

flying away. Even now, his final loyalty is to the old regime, not the new one.

And why not? His best years were the early years, when the Tigers still developed young talent, and when they had a pitching staff that scared something besides birds. That seems like a long time ago. Anderson, who always has been many things here—philosopher, historian, salesman, vaudeville act—has never had a year like this one.

It began with him walking away from the game—over his refusal to manage replacement players—and ends with him walking away from the franchise, after 84 losses in 144 games.

There was a night back in April when I interviewed Anderson as he waited for a call from the Tigers. The strike had ended, the players were headed to spring training, but Anderson still wasn't sure whether he had a job. This is a man who has won more games than all but two managers in the history of baseball.

I listened to him say, "If they don't call me, they don't call me. I'm prepared."

Truth is, he was embarrassed. And that was the beginning of the end.

Now he finished getting dressed, leggings, pants, belt. I asked whether he planned on taking anything from this year, any souvenir or keepsake.

"The hat," he said.

"That's it?"

"That's it."

The hat?

• • • • • • • • • • • • • • •

Sparky acknowledges the crowd from the dugout before one of his final home games during the 1995 season.

Outside the office, Tigers players were dressing for the final game of the season. There was a buzz in the room, like the last day of school. Players exchanged phone numbers and talked about tee times.

Against the far wall, Alan Trammell signed some baseballs. Sunday would be his last game, too. He and Lou Whitaker had played nearly every moment of their major league careers for Anderson.

"I'll be there for his press conference," Trammell said. "It'll be weird; it'll be emotional, but I can't miss it. I feel like I should be there."

Trammell was asked whether he thought the Tigers could have done anything to keep Anderson. He grinned sarcastically.

"I think," he said, "this is what Sparky wants."

Indeed it is. Anderson knows he still can manage. He also knows he can't spin gold from sawdust. It has been eight years since he has seen a post-season, 11 years since a World Series; he has maybe the worst pitching staff in baseball, few prospects on the horizon, and while he won't admit it, he is concerned that all this losing will cut into his historical glow. Maybe one day, they won't yell "you're a legend" anymore.

And when you are one, that hurts.

So Anderson will check out. On Sunday he even laid the ground rules for his next team—should there be one.

"I don't want to go to any rebuilding project. Oh, no. No more. I'd like to go back to winning some games. Having some victories would be nice. But I would only manage again under my conditions."

Which are?

"I have complete say in my coaches, that's No. 1. I keep who I want on my team, and I don't have to keep nobody I don't want. Nobody interferes with my clubhouse, and nobody"—he points around his office—"nobody calls me here."

What he means is, no owner interference. Nobody telling him who to pitch, who to trade, what he thinks should be happening. In other words, Sparky won't be working for George Steinbrenner.

Why should he?

• • • • • • • • • • • • • • • • • •

Sparky Anderson was honored along with Bo Schembechler, who had been head coach of the University of Michigan Football team for 20 years, by the Detroit Sports Broadcasters Association at the Detroit Press Club.

Now game time is just 90 minutes away.

"I need to get my boys in here," he said.

By this he meant Trammell, Whitaker, Cecil Fielder, Travis Fryman and John Doherty. Those players had been with him the longest.

"They deserve a private meeting."

One by one they came in, Fielder, his arms thick as a longshoreman, and Doherty, showing a pitcher's tan, and Trammell and Whitaker and Fryman, still in his underwear. And they shut the door and they sat down one more time. A few minutes later they emerged. This, in part, is what Sparky had told them:

"I haven't always said it… but I want you to know how much I appreciate the way you've played and acted like professionals."

He also told them he was leaving.

There goes ol' Silver Hair.

How can we gauge what he did since he was hired as Tigers manager in 1979? He won a World Series and more games than any Tigers manager in history. He took a ragtag team in 1987 and churned it into a division winner, giving Detroit arguably its best week of baseball ever, seven games, all against Toronto, all decided by one run, the last being the clincher, when Frank Tanana got the last man to ground out and Sparky actually ran from the dugout and kissed his pitcher in celebration.

"That may be the sweetest moment I had here," he admitted.

There were other not-so-sweet moments, the time in 1989 that he left in the middle of the season—family concerns—and all the outlandish predictions he made for rookies that never came true. (Remember Chris Pittaro?) And the last seven years, as he said Sunday, were mostly dismal: 495 wins, 574 losses, never finishing higher than a second-place tie.

But remember, baseball is not football or basketball. You don't win because you have elaborate schemes or unbelievable motivation. You win when you have top pitching and solid defense and menacing hitting. In other words, talent. He hasn't had a lot of it recently.

• • • • • • • • • • • • • • • • •

When the game started Sunday, Anderson was determined not to make a fuss. This, after all, was Camden Yards, not Tiger Stadium. He came out to deliver the lineup, and suddenly, in the stands behind home plate, fans began to clap.

Anderson, with his back to the crowd, had no idea what was happening.

Finally, he turned and ran back to the dugout, as the applause swelled into the upper deck, a standing ovation. Anderson glanced up before disappearing.

"Why didn't you walk back?" coach Dick Tracewski asked Sparky in the dugout.

"I didn't know they were clapping for me," he said.

He should have no such doubt today in Detroit. Love him or hate him, the man deserves a slap of appreciation. Sure, he was bloated with hot air, but he always took the game seriously, he fought for players he believed in, and he was beloved by the ones who truly understood the

Affectionately known as ol' Silver Hair, Sparky Anderson managed the Tigers during a golden era for the team.

sport. He was always kind to kids, was accessible to the media—heck, he was salvation to the media—and took criticism as part of the job.

He never took a good team and made it bad, although he did the reverse more than once during his tenure.

In the locker room after Sunday's game—fittingly, another loss—he sat for the last time by his desk, his white hair now matted with sweat. His uniform was already in the laundry. Sparky had not asked for it.

Only the hat.

"Do you have any thoughts on your career at this moment?" a Baltimore TV man asked.

"Yeah," Anderson said. "I'd like to know where all the years went."

They went into a legacy that will not soon be repeated. The truth is, as long as the Tigers had Sparky, they had star power. Now they become one of the nobody pack, another young team with marketing execs.

There goes ol' Silver Hair.

A few days ago, with the season long since dead, Sparky took a young pitcher into his office and chewed him out for his behavior on the mound. The next day, he pulled the kid aside and said, "I want you to know something. I did that because you needed it if you ever wanted to be great."

Maybe a few years from now, the kid will appreciate that kind of managing.

Maybe, a few years from now, we will, too. ●

Sparky Anderson takes time to hug Ann Drysdale, widow of Hall of Fame pitcher Don Drysdale, before a Tigers-Angels game on Opening Day in 1995.

By JOHN LOWE
Detroit Free Press
First published: Monday, July 24, 2000

The Hall of Fame

A fitting ending for a most worthy career, Sparky was enshrined in Baseball's Hall of Fame after a memorable speech

When the magnificent orator got to the podium Sunday, he pushed his notes to one side. "If I use notes," he said later, "I can't speak." So once again sailing without a map, he made what he called his final speech. In doing so, he wound up just where he started, in a small town.

He was born in a place where he says the population was 600—Bridgewater, S.D. He showed up there 66 years ago as George Lee Anderson.

Sunday, when he strode to the podium to receive his sport's highest honor, he did so in another small town: Cooperstown, N.Y., pop. 2,200.

He had accomplished enough in places bigger than Bridgewater that when baseball commissioner Bud Selig turned the microphone over to him, he could refer to him simply by his nickname:

"Sparky, welcome to the Hall of Fame."

The thousands in attendance rose to give Anderson a standing ovation.

"Please sit down," he said over the applause. "At ballparks, when they stand up, they're getting ready to boo. So just set it on down."

The crowd, estimated at 20,000, immediately went quiet and sat down. Anderson unfurled a 16-minute speech that reminded everyone of his spellbinding skills: the reverent voice, the memory for con-

Sparky Anderson was inducted into the Baseball Hall of Fame in Cooperstown, New York, in 2000.

AP IMAGES

GEORGE LEE ANDERSON
"SPARKY"
CINCINNATI, N.L., 1970-1978
DETROIT, A.L., 1979-1995
ONE OF THE GAME'S MOST SUCCESSFUL AND COLORFUL MANAGERS, HIS 2,194 WINS RANK THIRD IN HISTORY BEHIND CONNIE MACK AND JOHN McGRAW. THE CRANK THAT TURNED THE BIG RED MACHINE, HIS SKILLFUL LEADERSHIP HELPED THOSE CINCINNATI TEAMS DOMINATE IN THE 1970s. REVERED AND TREASURED BY HIS PLAYERS FOR HIS HUMILITY, HUMANITY, ETERNAL OPTIMISM AND KNOWLEDGE OF THE GAME. BASEBALL'S ONLY MANAGER TO WIN A WORLD SERIES IN BOTH LEAGUES AND LEAD TWO FRANCHISES IN VICTORIES. HIS TEAMS WON THREE WORLD SERIES, SEVEN DIVISION TITLES AND FIVE PENNANTS, COMPILING A .619 POST-SEASON WINNING PERCENTAGE.

versations and anecdotes, the ability to take you into his world.

His talk contained all of his vintage ingredients of oratory: respect and honor, humor and humility.

The high point came when he recalled something his father, LeRoy, told him when he was 11.

"My father never got past the third grade," Anderson said, "but there ain't a guy that ever went to Harvard as smart as my daddy.

"My daddy said this: 'I want to give you a gift, the greatest gift to take all the way through your life. If you live with this gift, everything will work perfect.'

"And he said, 'Son, I'm going to give you a gift that will never cost a dime. And that gift is this: If every day of your life, and every person you meet, you will just be nice to that person, and treat that person like they are someone.'"

He had used an incomplete sentence to complete his thought. Vintage Sparky.

"My daddy was all man," Anderson said. "He didn't need no big degrees to walk tall. He could walk tall just from the way he handled himself."

Through 26 years of big-league managing, Anderson probably gave a speech every day. Sometimes it was to an audience of one, be it a player or a reporter. Sometimes it was to a handful of reporters. And sometimes, if the writer was taking notes or a microphone was present, then he would be speaking to thousands of fans.

Sunday, he realized anew that he would never do that again. A manager must be retired to enter the Hall of Fame. Anderson hasn't managed since bowing out of Tiger Stadium after the '95 season. But Sunday's induction brought home to him that he's gone for good.

"This is the last time I'll ever get to speak," he said. "When I walk away from here today, I'll never win another game and lose another game. So in that respect it's a sad moment for me, knowing I will

Sparky Anderson's legacy will live on in Detroit thanks to his CATCH (Caring Athletes for Children's and Henry Ford Hospital) foundation. He used his 60th birthday party in 1994 as a way to raise funds for the organization.

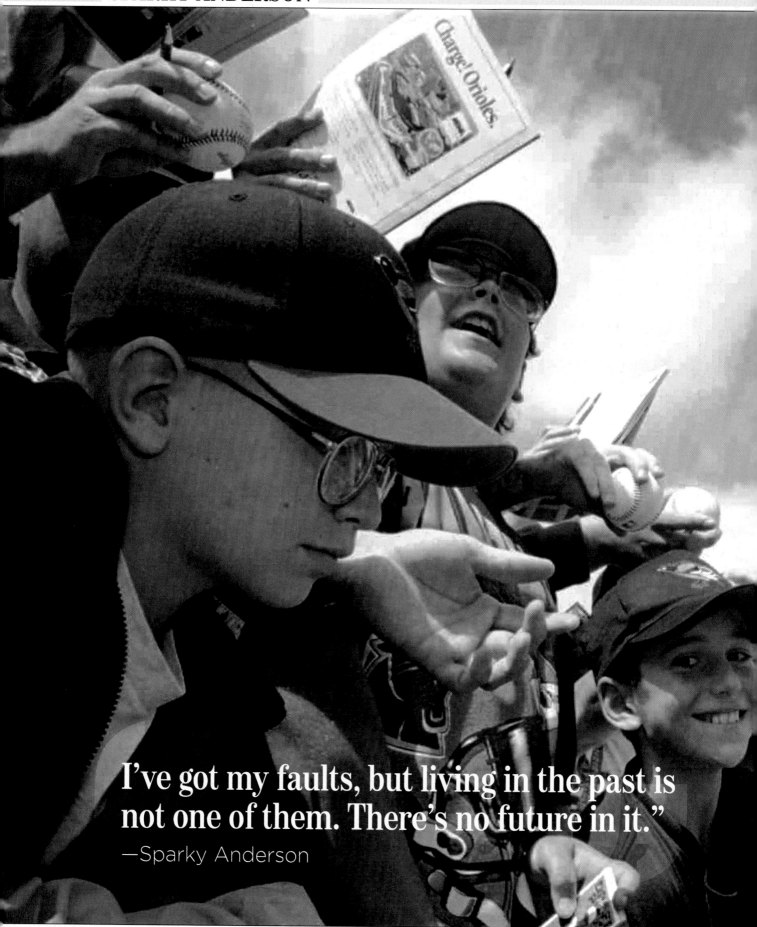

I've got my faults, but living in the past is not one of them. There's no future in it."
—Sparky Anderson

never get to get up in front of a group."

Unlike his managerial contemporary Tom Lasorda, Anderson doesn't enjoy traveling to speak. So it looks as if Anderson's future speeches will come only when he's sitting around with his friends at the golf course in his home of Thousand Oaks, Calif.

The amazing part of Anderson's daily speeches over the years was they were all off-the-cuff. Even when he gave formal addresses, he didn't believe in using notes. To make sure he didn't miss anyone important Sunday, he had notes written on pieces of paper about the size of index cards.

"I spent five months working on them," he said after the ceremony, holding the unused notes in his hand.

Anderson never broke down during his speech. Even more remarkably, given this culmination-of-career setting, he took only one wrong turn in his talk, said only one thing that made him correct himself. It came when he referred to a former president as "the late George Bush."

Thus, Sparky continued to keep oratorical pace with his fellow Hall of Fame manager Casey Stengel. Ol' Case once said of someone, "He is dead at the present time."

Sparky might think his speaking career is dead at the present time. But I think he deserves to make an acceptance speech at another Hall of Fame: The Orators Hall of Fame. ●

Even in his final season managing, Sparky had no problem letting an umpire know he saw something differently. Here John Higgins is on the receiving end of Sparky explaining what he saw happen at first base in the Kingdome when the Tigers were facing the Mariners in 1995.

AP IMAGES

By JO-ANN BARNAS
Detroit Free Press
First published: Sunday, Aug. 27, 2006

Sparky in Retirement

Never one to sit still, Sparky kept on firing long after he stepped down from the Tigers

It's still dark at 5:35 a.m. in Sparky Anderson's neighborhood. Streetlights illuminate the bend in the road near his home, casting a glow on the flowers in his yard—pink and fuchsia climbing geraniums, yellow and orange marigolds. The envy of the block, he will tell you.

The first few minutes after waking up is the only hectic period of Anderson's day. He moves quietly so he won't disturb Carol, his wife of 52 years.

Anderson has kicked off most mornings this way since 1999, four years after retiring from managing the Tigers, when amid his recovery from heart-bypass surgery he embraced a routine that he says has enhanced his life more than baseball ever did.

You know this because at 5:37 a.m., Anderson is standing in his driveway. He unscrews the cap from a bottle filled with iced tea and takes a swig.

"Let's go for a walk," he says.

This is not just a baseball story.

Almost assuredly, fans in Detroit remember Anderson as the manager who led the Tigers to the 1984 World Series title.

In Cincinnati, he's revered for taking the Big Red Machine to the

Seen here at his Thousand Oaks, California, home in March of 1995, Sparky explained that he would not manage replacement players because it would compromise the integrity of the game.

1975 and 1976 championships.

But when Anderson looks in the mirror, he doesn't see baseball.

Not anymore.

He sees a 72-year-old grandfather of 15.

He sees a gardener.

He sees a golfer who likes chatting up new interests—politics and history—when he's "cheating with my boys" on the golf course.

He sees a husband fortunate for the chance to assume some of the household chores his wife took care of all those years he was managing. So Anderson happily pushes the grocery cart at Albertson's, where he knows every checker by name.

He sees a college sports fan with the best seat in the house—the dugout—for California Lutheran baseball games. The field, recently renamed in his honor, is around the corner from the home the Andersons have owned for 40 years.

And he sees a walker, which is where the next part of this story begins.

Five days a week at precisely 5:45 a.m., Anderson slides into the front seat of his 10-year-old white Crown Victoria (aka Tank) and drives a quarter-mile to a parking lot at California Lutheran University.

He recently had the car "fixed up a bit," he says. That means duct tape is no longer required to secure his rearview mirror to the windshield, or to hold together a cracked inside door panel on the driver's side of his car.

Anderson has a newer model Crown Vic in his garage but prefers driving Tank because it's "got a lot of heart," he says.

In the passenger seat on this day is Dan Ewald, the Tigers' former publicity manager and Anderson's close friend for nearly 30 years. Ewald, who lives in suburban Detroit, is in Thousand Oaks for the week visiting and helping Anderson around the house. This afternoon's job: clearing ivy from the fence line in back.

By 5:40 a.m., Ewald has already taken care of one of Anderson's rituals before beginning their walk around the university and surrounding neighborhoods. He has run up the morning newspaper from the driveways of Anderson's neighbors and placed them at their front doors.

Funny. When Anderson retired from managing 11 years ago, his wife worried about him.

"I'm an 'A' person," Anderson explains, referring to his competitive and work-obsessed persona he needed in baseball. "She didn't think I could" retire. "And when I did, it hadn't even been two weeks and she said, 'I've seen you change.'"

Anderson, head down, arms pumping, is on his second loop around Alumni Hall on campus. He's wearing white tennis shoes, white socks, blue shorts and a lightweight jacket over a white T-shirt. A beige cap with the words "Soule Park" is atop his thinning white hair.

Between 5:54 and 5:57 a.m., he says, he'll run into another walker, a woman named Shirley. And sure enough, here she comes toward them.

"Shirley's down pat," Anderson says with a smile.

Anderson already has waved to Joe, a campus security guard.

Sparky ponders a question addressed to him at a press conference in February of 2000 announcing that he had been voted into the Baseball Hall of Fame.

Heading toward a community garden in the lot behind a Lutheran church, Anderson picks up his pace before reaching his first stopping point.

"You have to look down—you never know where the boys are," he says, referring to rattlesnakes. Anderson wags a finger at rows of vegetables he helped cultivate this summer.

"Here are the cucumbers, Japanese," Anderson says. "And zucchini."

He points to flowers—yellow marigolds as bright as the sun. "These I plant, and they'll stay all summer. Here's cantaloupe and cherry tomatoes. I cleaned them out yesterday. I want to go with the beef tomatoes next year."

Back on the sidewalk, Anderson and Ewald are a few minutes from meeting up with Mary Imsland, 70, and Elaine Eickmeyer, 73, who also live in Thousand Oaks.

Anderson credits the retired schoolteachers, whom he fondly calls "my girls," for getting him hooked on walking.

He noticed the two women walking by his kitchen window when he was recuperating from heart surgery. His street was on their route.

When he was well enough, he began walking on his own and bumped into Imsland and Eickmeyer. He asked if he could join them. They didn't know who Anderson was at first.

He liked that.

Although Anderson was hospitalized in 2004 with a rheumatoid-related illness, he proclaims himself in good health now after a recent physical. Blood pressure: 126/70. Cholesterol: 126.

Weight: 143—"same as I weighed in high school, " he says.

He believes walking in the morning gives him energy for the rest of the day. Plus, Anderson just feels better.

"Baseball to me now was like a toy you play with," he says. "It was fun. That's all it is. Fun. But it's not life."

"Why does it take retirement to realize that?" he is asked.

Sparky Anderson can be seen here in the dugout before a home game against the Seattle Mariners in July of the strike-shortened 1994 season.

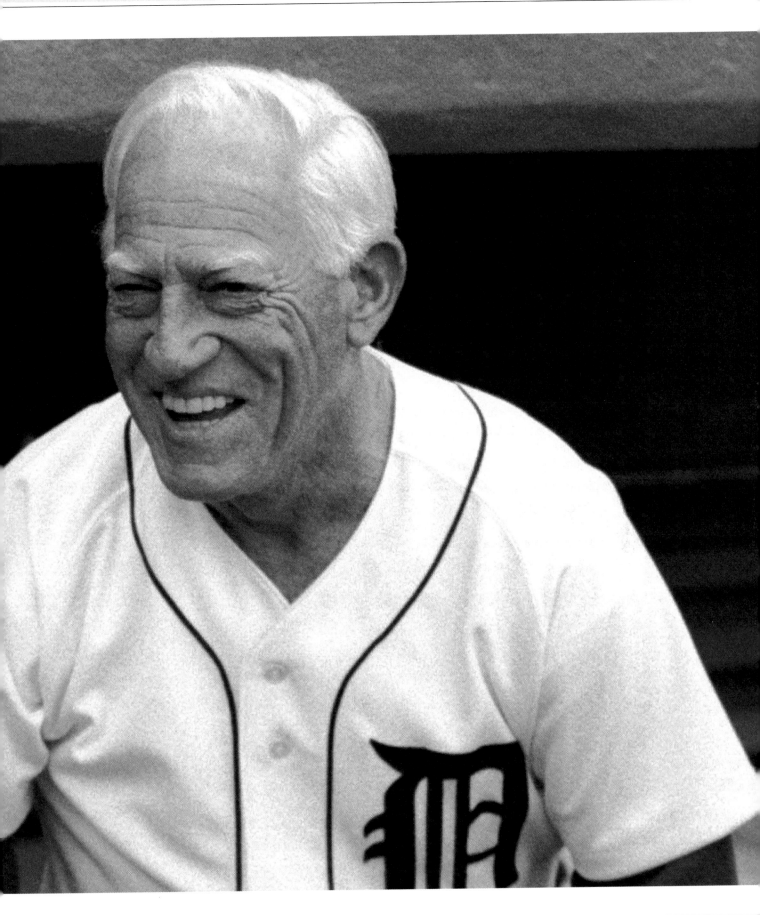

"Why did it take me to get ill?" Anderson says with a smile. "The biggest thing that young people can only learn is, do the best you can at what you do, and then when you're through with it, don't try to live it again. I don't live baseball anymore."

"You're more fulfilled," Ewald says.

"It's not even close," Anderson says. "Hey, there's Mary on the left, Ike on the right—6:15."

Nine minutes later, two more walkers join the group. Anderson, walking ahead, passes the Thousand Oaks Health Care Center, where a green sports car is parked at the curb out front.

"We call him Green Man," Anderson says. "He brings a little gift everyday for his wife. He comes and stays—I guess, Mary, he stays for about four hours?"

"I imagine," she says.

"He's a little old man with a rod for a car," Anderson continues. "But his wife, she's been here about 15, 16 months, and he comes to see her everyday. Can you imagine that?"

The group heads toward another neighborhood. Anderson has been walking for about an hour now.

He's asked about the 1984 Tigers, if he hears from his former players often.

"Not much," he says. "Dan Petry—which I always look forward to—Danny always calls me at Christmastime. He's such a good kid. I will never leave the game as far as the friendships, and what the game has done for so many people."

Has he spoken lately to Jim Leyland, the Tigers manager?

"No, no, Jimmy and me, I would hope, are friends," Anderson says. "There are friends and there are personal friends, and it's totally different. But that doesn't mean a guy running a ball club wants—I call them green flies—he doesn't need green flies coming around. He has work to do."

Is it easier or harder to manage when things are going well?

"At times it can be harder for this reason," Anderson says, bringing up this year's Tigers. "At this point right now, with the lead they have, just imagine if you lose it? That's the way I always looked at it. Like in '84, I told the coaches, 'Boys, I have news for you. If we don't win this, look at centerfield, on that flagpole. The flag won't be there, it will be me.' It's true. I don't care who you are. You don't take anything for granted when you're in it."

He's asked about Alan Trammell, star shortstop on that 1984 World Series team. Trammell was fired as Tigers manager after the 2005 season.

"I talked with Alan about six weeks ago," Anderson says. "He sounds good. I can tell you something that really sounds crazy: I love him. I've never been around a young man that knew how to be a professional like he was.

"I encouraged him to sit for a year. I said, 'Why come out with something that you feel bad about?' Just like me now—seven, eight years ago I was totally different. Now I look at everything clearer." Anderson returns to Michigan a couple of times a year, mostly for his golf tournament for a children's charity and speaking engagements. But he

Not only loved by his own players, players across the league, like Tony Peña of the Cleveland Indians, respected and appreciated what Sparky had done for the game of baseball.

hasn't been to Comerica Park since the year the stadium opened, he said.

"It's been awhile," he says. "But that's the way it should be."

Finished with their walk—total time: 1 hour, 35 minutes—Anderson and Ewald head back to the parking lot. Anderson fires up Tank.

On the way to a restaurant, Anderson spots a neighbor washing his car in the driveway. Anderson stops in front of the house, rolls down his window, and yells: "I have a writer here from Detroit. She wants to do a big profile on you. Do you have 20 seconds?"

He laughs, rolls up the window and speeds away.

At the restaurant, Anderson and Ewald choose a booth away from the door. A waitress—her name tag reads Bryonna—arrives at their table.

"Are you from France?" Anderson asks.

"No, I'm not," she replies.

"That's too bad," Anderson says. "I wanted to practice ordering in French."

More laughter.

He discusses some of the household duties he has inherited since he retired, such as gardening and sending out the Christmas cards.

Back when he managed, he says, Carol mailed almost 500 a year. Two years ago, Anderson cut the list down to 160 and started his own tradition: He sent the cards out after Christmas because he can buy them at half price.

But Anderson goofed last year. "I missed the sale," he says, "and didn't send them out."

Another laugh.

Don't let Anderson's seemingly frugal ways throw you off, Ewald says. His friend is a generous man.

Anderson takes his children and their spouses—Ewald, too—on a cruise every year. When he heard that a woman—an acquaintance of the family—lived in a rented garage, he bought carpeting and furniture after visiting her and had it delivered to her home.

Anderson still says "thank you" when he's asked for an autograph. Asked why, Anderson replies: "I'm from Bridgewater, S.D. Six hundred people lived in my town, and I'm the only person from there in the Hall of Fame. For that I say 'Thank you.'"

Anderson orders corned beef hash—"No eggs," he says—and raisin toast and fruit. He pours cream into his coffee. The waitress returns and refills his ice water.

"I drink water all the time," Anderson says.

His right hand trembles slightly as he spreads grape jelly on a piece of toast.

"Somebody said to me, 'You don't hurry no more,'" he says. "I said, 'I'll tell you why: I don't want to go there too quick.'"

Anderson nods toward the ground. You get the point.

"I asked Dan the other day, 'How does this all go on without us?'

"That's the one thing: You don't go on forever." ●

One season after retiring from managing the Detroit Tigers, Sparky was honored by Cincinnati when he was the Grand Marshall of the Reds Opening Day parade on April 1, 1996.

Sparky & Ernie

One Detroit baseball legend fondly discusses another

Editor's Note: Sparky Anderson and Hall of Fame broadcaster Ernie Harwell were fast friends during Anderson's tenure with the Tigers. Here's a column Harwell, who died May 4, 2010, wrote for the *Free Press* in July 2000.

Everybody has a Sparky Anderson story. I have two, and each reflects his human touch—one with his players and one with his public.

When Sparky's Reds played the Orioles in the 1970 World Series, he had a second-string catcher named Pat Corrales. In his third year of backing up Johnny Bench, Corrales was finishing the sixth year of his nine-year, undistinguished career.

The Orioles were leading the series, three games to one. The final game at Baltimore's Memorial Stadium found the Birds ahead, 9-3, in the ninth. It was all over—just a matter of three more outs.

Mike Cueller retired the first two Reds easily. One to go and the Orioles were champions.

Corrales was watching from the dugout. It was his first World Series and his last. Anderson looked down the bench toward Corrales.

"Pat," he told him, "get up there and hit for Hal McRae. You deserve to be in a World Series, and this might be your only chance."

Corrales grounded out to third baseman Brooks Robinson, and the series was over. But he had batted in a World Series—thanks to a thoughtful manager.

My other Anderson story happened in 1984, the year the Tigers started 35-5. Sparky's team had won 16 road games in a row. His picture graced the covers of magazines, and his name was in headlines across the country.

He and I were having breakfast at our Anaheim, Calif., hotel when a fan approached our table.

"Hi, Sparky," he said. "I'm a great fan of yours. I live in San Diego now, but I was living in Cincinnati when you managed that Big Red Machine. You have always been my hero. Without a doubt you are the greatest manager ever."

Sparky beamed. Silently, he listened and just nodded his head. Then, the man spoke again.

"And by the way, Sparky, what are you doing these days?"

Sparky gave him a polite smile and returned to his eggs and bacon. But that fan's question gave Anderson a conversation topic for the rest of the trip.

Sparky always understood the mind of the baseball fan and the player. ●

The Detroit Tigers lost two legendary members of their family in 2010 with the passing of long time broadcaster Ernie Harwell and former manager Sparky Anderson.

SPARKY ANDERSON
HIS LIFE AND TIMES

Name: George Lee (Sparky) Anderson.

Born: Bridgewater, S.D., Feb. 22, 1934.

Died: Thousand Oaks, Calif., Nov. 4, 2010.

Family: Wife, Carol; sons Lee and Albert; daughter Shirley Englebrecht.

CAREER HIGHLIGHTS

- Elected to Hall of Fame in 2000, the 16th manager so honored.

- First manager to win 100 games in a season with two franchises.

- First manager to win 800 games with two franchises.

- First manager to win a World Series in both leagues.

- Only manager to lead two franchises in victories (Detroit, 1,331 and Cincinnati, 863).

- Led 1984 Tigers to club record 104 victories.

- First on Tigers' all-time managers list with 1,331 victories and 2,579 games.

- Voted manager of the year in American (1984, 1987) and National (1972, 1975) leagues.

- Ranks sixth in all-time victories among major league managers.

- Career record of 2,194-1,834 (.545) and Tigers record of 1,331-1,248 (.516).

- Played one season in the major leagues, hitting .218 with no home runs and 34 RBIs in 152 games with the Philadelphia Phillies in 1959.

- Became Tigers manager June 12, 1979. First game in uniform was June 14.

- Resigned after 1995 season. Last game in uniform was Oct. 1.

- Decided his Hall of Fame plaque would show him in a Reds caps because "I had no choice. Bob Howsam gave me a job at the age of 35. I thought he was crazy. I think the world thought he was crazy."